Aiko's Journey

Part One

MIRIAM M. BATTS

Miriam M. Batts
March, 2005

TRAFFORD
• Canada • UK • Ireland • USA •

© Copyright 2004, Miriam M. Batts.
All rights reserved.
No part of this publication may be reproduced, stored in a retrieval system, or transmitted, in any form or by any means, electronic, mechanical, photocopying, recording, or otherwise, without the written prior permission of the author.

Note for Librarians: a cataloguing record for this book that includes Dewey Decimal Classification and US Library of Congress numbers is available from the Library and Archives of Canada. The complete cataloguing record can be obtained from their online database at: www.collectionscanada.ca/amicus/index-e.html
ISBN 1-4120-4430-8
Printed in Victoria, BC, Canada

TRAFFORD

Offices in Canada, USA, Ireland, UK
This book was published *on-demand* in cooperation with Trafford Publishing. On-demand publishing is a unique process and service of making a book available for retail sale to the public taking advantage of on-demand manufacturing and Internet marketing. On-demand publishing includes promotions, retail sales, manufacturing, order fulfilment, accounting and collecting royalties on behalf of the author.

Books sales in Europe:
Trafford Publishing (UK) Ltd., Enterprise House, Wistaston Road Business Centre, Wistaston Road,
Crewe CW2 7RP UNITED KINGDOM
phone 01270 251 396 (local rate 0845 230 9601)
facsimile 01270 254 983; orders.uk@trafford.com

Book sales for North America and international:
Trafford Publishing, 6E–2333 Government St.,
Victoria, BC V8T 4P4 CANADA
phone 250 383 6864 (toll-free 1 888 232 4444)
fax 250 383 6804; email to orders@trafford.com

Order online at:
www.trafford.com/robots/04-2238.html

10 9 8 7 6 5 4 3 2

Acknowledgment

At first I was not going to write any acknowledgment. As I went on reading, however, to make the corrections, I felt a deep desire to acknowledge my parents and thank them for having been my parents. How perfect they were with all their imperfections!

My father, unlike other Oriental men, had liberated democratic ideas. He was open to women's education and advancement in life. Without a father with such ideas, I would not have been able to go to universities and my life would have been totally different.

My father had a great sense of humour and an explosive Korean temperament.

My mother was a compassionate woman and any cruelty upset her. She was a skilled sewer and always kept us, her children, in nice clothes she made. She cultivated the flair I have for dresses. The fact that she came from a wealthy family enabled her to distinguish the genuine from the fake. She was adamant about keeping the standard of life.

Both of my parents had one thing in common, generosity. They were always giving even when we ourselves did not have much. Their examples taught us much about generosity.

I am what I am because of what my parents were. I am proud to be a mixture of Korean and Japanese for I have inherited unique traits of the two races. Hereby I would like to express my thanks to them.

Foreword

This is part one of the life story of a woman, who was born of Korean-Japanese descent in Japan, during the Japanese Annexation of Korea. Most people do not know about the suffering of the Koreans, who endured the Japanese oppression for 36 years. The author had lived, without a passport, for over twenty years, due to the Japanese policy of not recognizing Koreans as fully-fledged Japanese citizens. Even now, the Koreans, who were born in Japan to the parents who had emigrated during the Annexation period, are living in Japan without any definite nationality. They number approximately 600,000. This story is, however, not just a narration of personal experiences but also a record of the social experiences of ordinary people during the period from the 1920s to the end of World War II in 1945.

The journey will continue.

chapter 1

I was born in Yokohama, Japan, in 1929, the year the Great Depression started and 19 years after Japan annexed Korea, as a second daughter to a Korean father and a Japanese mother. Japan, in the late 19th century, woke up from a two-hundred-and-seventy-year long secluded dream to a world where western white powers dominated. Japan was quick to realize what was urgently needed to make it an equal to the world powers. Japan poured its energy into industrializing the country and building up a strong army and navy. In order to build up a strong army and navy, the country needed strong young men. Under the policy of the new government, the population increased rapidly. Japan needed raw materials and the land to expand. It was the age of Imperialism. Great Britain had boasted that the sun never set in its empire because it possessed so many colonies. Japan was envious. It wanted to be like Great Britain. In fact, it was imitating Great Britain in many ways of life. In order to acquire colonies, to where could Japan expand? To Korea, its weak neighbour.

Korea, the unfortunate neighbour, had not kept up with the modernization of the country. The royal family was weak and had neither the foresight nor the strength to fend off the strong enemy that coveted the country. China, which had been a sort of protector, was defeated by Japan in 1895. Russia, which had an interest in Manchuria, was defeated by Japan in 1905. The feeble resistance put up by the Korean pro-Russian empress dowager was easily quashed by her assassination by the Japanese. Korea was annexed; the royal family was abolished. The last crown prince of the Lee dynasty was brought to Japan and made a Japanese prince. The Japanese Prime Minister, Hirobumi Ito, who realized the annexation of Korea, was later assassinated by a Korean at the Harbin railway station in Manchuria.

The Korean crown prince was engaged at the time to a Korean noble woman but the Japanese paid no regard to the engagement and simply carried the prince away to Japan. In Korea, once a woman was engaged, she had no right to look for another man. Afterwards, no one knew what actually became of this lady.

Once Japan got a hold of Korea, it suppressed this supposedly inferior country with an iron fist. They forbade the use of the Korean native tongue, took away all the opportunities of their advancement in life, imposed the Japanese way of life upon them and laughed at the imperfect Japanese Koreans were forced to speak and the smell of garlic Koreans favoured in their diet. The harshness of the rule caused the Koreans to revolt in 1917 but the revolt was quickly put down. They tried to fight without weapons against the armed Japanese. Hundreds of Koreans were arrested, tortured and killed. One Korean girl of 17 was tortured to such an extent that her face was unrecognizable. Nobody dared to go to the Japanese police to claim her body out of fear of retaliation by the Japanese. Finally, a British female missionary went to claim her.

My father was 17 years old but was one of the ringleaders in the area where he lived. He was arrested and put in prison. After six months of living in horrible conditions, he was released. Emperor Meiji died and general amnesty was declared. Another fortunate fact was that my father was a minor. Crimes committed by minors were not officially recorded. He was just put on the black list and had to be watched. So a Tokko (special police department dealing with political affairs) detective would trail after him but no record would be put down on paper. They eventually stopped following him altogether sometime after my father married a Japanese woman and had children. Little did they know about the soul of a man who loved his country. In the initial period of my parents' marriage, the Japanese police was still suspicious. One snowy night, my mother noticed a Tokko detective standing outside keeping watch. White snow was falling upon the dark hat and shoulders of a man clad in a cheap suit and an overcoat. My mother was a compassionate woman. She went out and said to him, "Won't you come in? It's cold out here." "Thank you, madam", he replied. "This is my duty. I will stay here."

One of the measures the Japanese took against the Koreans was to take away opportunities for education. Since Koreans were second-rate human beings, they would not need education. The Japanese school in Seoul did not accept Korean children. The University of Seoul, which was a branch university of the Imperial University in Tokyo, did not allow Koreans to enroll. Since dangerous ideology starts at universities, Koreans had better be kept ignorant. However, my father had an insatiable desire to study. Education was the only way to advance himself over the Japanese. Since the Japanese took away almost every means of earning a decent livelihood, almost every Korean was poor and my father's family was no exception. There was no money and there was no school he could attend. He tried to travel to Manchuria first. It was in the dead of winter. He was thinly clad without an overcoat. Fortunately, his family sent a relative to look for him and he was rescued from a train before he froze to death. Ironically, the opportunity to study existed only in Japan. By then, hordes of Koreans had immigrated to Japan, seeking work and food. They were excluded from any decent jobs, so they worked at the jobs which the Japanese shunned and despised. One of the jobs they could find was carrying buckets of night soils (most Japanese households had no flush toilet).

After arriving in Japan, my father found a job in the kitchen of a very famous bakery, Nakamuraya. The wife of the bakery's owner was an ardent supporter of the Indian independence movement. So she was also sympathetic to the Koreans. Since it was a confectionery's kitchen, there were always some leftovers or sub-standards. While the other workers devoured them, my father would not touch them. He had a lofty philosophy that anybody who wanted to make something out of himself should not indulge himself in eating someone else's leftovers.

Eventually he managed to enter Yokohama Koko, a college where a lot of brains came to study. This college later became the University of Kanagawa. Although the Korean language is quite similar to Japanese, it is a foreign language and he had a scanty middle school background. But he passed the entrance examinations placing fifth. His educated friends had no prejudices. During the great earthquake of 1923, the Japanese spread a rumour that the Koreans were poisoning wells. In those days, a large number of households, even in Tokyo, drew water from wells. Some two hundred Koreans were massacred by being stabbed with bamboo spears just because they could not pronounce Japanese words properly which disclosed that they were Korean. The Tokko (special intelligence) came to the college to look for any Koreans at the school. My father's fellow students sent the officer away by telling him that there were no Koreans there.

During his college days, he got married and my elder sister arrived after a year. Since he had to pay for his schooling and support his family, he started to work as well as going to college. He was frequently absent from his classes. His major was electrical science so experiments were required. When his friends discovered that he was away for work, they would set up his implements for the experiments on his desk so that when the professor came around, it would look as if he was also doing the work.

In the year the Great Depression began, he had two things: a graduation diploma and a new baby. Now that he had a post-secondary diploma, getting a job was easier. Also, as a result of the 1917 uprising, the Japanese government relaxed the rules slightly and tried to assimilate Koreans into Japanese society and some companies were advised to hire a certain percentage of Koreans. All these facts added up and my father managed to get a job at Oki Denki, a prestigious electric company.

This was a relatively peaceful period for my family. My father had a steady income and Japan itself had not started any wars, although the seeds of the Great War were already sown by the Japanese invasion of Manchuria in 1931. I was living in this warm atmosphere. The house my parents rented had a garden big enough for my elder sister and me to play in. It had a small mound at the end for landscape purposes. The average Japanese houses for renters usually consisted of a few rooms: "hachijo" (eight tatami mats), "rokujo" (six tatami mats) and "yonotjohan" (four and a half tatami mats). Sometimes it also had a "sanjo" (three mats) room. Houses were not built directly on the ground but raised up about 1 and ½ yards from the ground, so the air could go through and the ventilation would prevent the houses from rotting since Japan is a very humid country. One side of the house faced the yard. Along the rooms that faced the yard, there was a stretch of boarded area, called "engawa". At one end of the "engawa", there was storage for wooden shutters and the shutters were slid in and out one by one. At night, they were pulled out to enclose the room that faced the garden. In the morning, the first task one had to perform was to slide the shutters back into the storage area to open up the room. Children often were in charge of shutters.

The world was more peaceful in general. Although Japanese houses were quite open, they were not locked unless the whole family went out for a while. Not many big crimes were committed. The militaristic government had a firm grip of the country and the Japanese police was famous for its efficiency. Policemen wore a sabre and could stop anyone at any time for questioning. A man and a woman walking together might become the subjects of questioning because this kind of togetherness was highly immoral. Once, a young man was stopped by a policeman and was interrogated because he happened to be carrying a woman's kimono. But this meant that crimes were few. People behaved out of fear. The punishment was severe and often the innocent were tortured to obtain a false confession.

While my sister and I played, my mother cleaned the house. When she worked around the house, she would wear a white apron that would cover the whole front, hike up the hem of her kimono and cover her hair with a "tenugui" (Japanese hand towel). Now this "engawa" had to be wiped clean using a bucket of water and a rag. Then it had to be waxed and polished. Sometimes she polished it so well, it shone and we could skate on it. After the cleaning, she would sit in one of the rooms facing the garden and sew. Prior to the end of World War II in 1945, all women had to be able to cook, sew and be good at housekeeping. Equally, all women had to get married. If any woman unfortunately remained unmarried at 23, she was labelled "old Miss" and looked down upon socially. A few enlightened women, who dared to defy the rule, "wasted time" on reading and went on to receive higher education, were laughed at and few men wanted to marry such women because they were too educated and too intimidating.

My mother was the youngest of three daughters born to a colonel in the Japanese army. The daughters were orphaned when my mother was only three years old. Her father was once stationed in Formosa and his second daughter, my aunt, was born there. The family obviously was destined to have some relationship with countries other than Japan.

My mother's recollection of her father was that every morning a private came round with a horse to take him to the office. My mother's family registration place used to be in Yotsuya, where many former feudal lords had their residences that had walls and big gates. After the restoration of power to the emperor in 1868, the lords dispersed but a few of them remained in the same area. One of them was Lord Naito. His descendant became a doctor and was practicing at his private clinic in the area.

At the time my mother was orphaned, one of her female cousins had been married for several years but the couple had no children. The female cousin had been working at Prince Fushimi's palace before her marriage. In those days, quite a few families sent their daughters to a household of a higher ranking person so that they could learn some manners. I don't know why her family kept her there so long but when she finished her term and came home, she was already 23 years old. As it looked as though she was going to be a grand old maid, her male cousin came to visit and he brought a friend.

For some unknown reason my step-grandfather fell madly in love with her. He abruptly changed his life style. Hitherto he had spent time fooling around with geishas. He gave up all the women he had known before and after the marriage, he would not even glance at another woman. "All women are the same" was his enlightened philosophy. When I met my maternal step-grandmother, I did not understand what was so attractive about her but she certainly seemed to have a nice character.

When my mother became orphaned it was the husband who was eager to adopt her. He loved the baby and doted on her. My step-grandfather had no higher education; in those days, only a few had a post-secondary education. He was a wholesaler of straw mats used for packing.

The adopting of an orphan brought good luck. By sheer coincidence, he got to know a man who worked at Nichinichi Sinbun (Nichi-nichi Newspaper) and his business started booming. Straw mats were in great demand for they were needed for all packing as protective wrapping. He was prosperous. He owned the land around what is today Ebisu railway station. In the same area, he owned houses which he rented.

He pampered my mother by buying her expensive things. For her trousseau, he filled up the drawers of chests with expensive kimonos. He bought her a five-yen umbrella while an ordinary umbrella cost only one yen. One thing he did not approve of was sending a girl to a higher educational institution than "joggakko", the equivalent of five-year French lycée. But he did believe in learning a trade, just in case. In those days, women could not go to co-ed universities anyway. A higher education for women meant going to a three-year college. That three-year college education was for "just in case". It was considered to be unfortunate if a woman had to use it and fend for herself. The ideal was a good husband who would remain alive and support the family.

So my step-grandfather sent her to a sewing teacher. After the first day of the lesson, he asked her: "What did you do today?"

"Oh, all the girls talked about actors."

On the second day he asked the same question: "What did you do today?"

"We talked about actors again."

On the third day after hearing the same answer, he said: "That's enough. Now you go to a professional."

The majority of girls came to a sewing teacher as part of a finishing school. The other subjects those girls were supposed to be learning were: the tea ceremony, flower arrangement, cooking and manners. But none of them took the study very seriously. They were merely filling in time until a husband came along.

The subjects the young girls half-heartedly learned rarely sustained them when they were left alone without a husband. My step-grandfather believed in serious learning. So, my mother was apprenticed to a professional kimono maker. Since she was paying tuition and went home everyday, she did not have to get up early in the morning, scrub the floor with cold water, help with the baby, if there was one, and usually there was, endure the wife's harsh words, evade sexual innuendo wisely, until the day when the teacher felt benevolent enough to throw an unmade kimono sleeve at her with a curt order of "Make it." No tradesman would have taught an apprentice with pampering words of "You cut it this like this and you make it so," etc. One was supposed to be all ears and eyes to absorb the words and gestures of the teacher directed to the more advanced apprentices.

Every day, shine or rain, my step-grandfather would wait by the front door with the sewing box so that my mother would not skip a class. On the way to the kimono shop, she had to cut through the premises of a Buddhist temple. One day, she noticed a young nice-looking parish priest standing there watching her. For a whole year, like a faithful watchdog, he came out to see my mother. Then he proposed. If she had accepted, he would have gone to speak to my step-grandfather. This would have been a good proposal because being a Buddhist priest's wife is a respected position. But my mother had to decline.

In those days, people were not allowed to let a family become extinct. If there was only one girl in the family, she had to marry a man who was willing enough to give up his own family name and take up her family name. This was a very difficult thing to do. Most proud decent males were not willing to do this and it limited my mother's choice of a husband.

My mother hated the atmosphere of the shop where she took sewing lessons. All the kimono makers were males and the subjects of their conversation were not cultured. They constantly cracked dirty jokes and they grated on her nerves. Even though she was paying tuition, she was not more pampered than the live-in apprentices. She, too, had to sit there observing, listening and learning. One day the teacher would throw her a part of a kimono -the starting piece is a sleeve—and she would have to make it up. If he liked the finished product, he would put it away without a compliment. If the product was not satisfactory, he would rip it apart in cold cutting silence. My mother was talented and advanced within a few years to the stage where she could sew for the clients of the shop. The shop owner liked this extra hand for which he did not have to pay wages.

The owner of the shop, who had been her teacher, was afraid that if he taught her everything and given her a diploma, she would leave and he would lose this useful seamstress. So, he held back the last subject, a man's pantaloons. Three months had passed when my step-grandfather lost patience.

"Quit it," he ordered, "You don't need a diploma."

She was his only child and would inherit all the money he had. She would never have to earn her living.

My mother's sewing box was a magical box for me. It was about 17 inches high, 13 inches long and about seven inches wide. The top had a lid and when it flipped open, there were a pin cushion, thimble, different sizes of needles (Japanese needles had tiny little eyes) and at one side of the box, there was a slit to stand up a ruler. On one side of the sewing box, there were little drawers that had metal handles that clanked when I opened them. There lay coloured tapes, laces, snaps, hooks and other little items that were necessary for sewing. My mother made all the clothes, some western style and some traditional kimonos, for my sister and me. She kept us so nice looking that she was often complimented. In those days, there were a lot of things to sew for women. Most women were still wearing traditional kimonos. Besides making those, they had to clean them themselves. Good silk kimonos required professional care but kimonos of lesser quality had to be taken apart, washed by hand and stretched out to dry, piece by piece on a long wooden board, called "hari-ita". When the pieces were dry, they had to be sewn back together as a kimono.

Women also had to make futons (beddings) and clean them. Once a year, the cover was opened, the cotton batting was taken out and sent away to the shop where it was cleaned and puffed up again. I dreaded the day when the batting came back and my mother had to put it back into the cover. In order to put it back in the cover, one laid the cover on the floor with the wrong side up. Then one placed the batting on the top of it, rolled up the four corners and turned the whole thing inside out. Since it was more advantageous to roll up the four corners all at once, we children were summoned to perform the duty and I hated the housework. I also dreaded the days when my mother cleaned the "shoji" screens or made "ohagi" (sweet cakes, made of hard rice and covered with sweet mashed red beans). I hated the unsettled atmosphere caused by busy movements and the loss of my reading time. Since I proved to be pretty useless at housekeeping tasks, I was often exempted from them. My sister, who was good at such things, was relied upon and I was dismissed. But all the knowledge of housekeeping, sewing and cooking seeped into my brain and became useful later.

Life was generally peaceful in those days. But it was in those days that I sensed that there was something different about us. I was not old enough to grasp this vague feeling but soon it took a concrete form. One of the neighbours did not want her children to play with Korean children. My mother was crushed. My mother was crushed every time someone said "Koreans." I think it was because she had no Korean blood in her.

I would get upset if someone called me Korean not because I was insulted for being Korean but I was mad at their ignorance and stupidity. I believe in the Buddhist theory of reincarnation. One must have had a past life before one was born for this particular span of life. I knew a lot of things at an early age without being taught. Even as a child, I knew that racism was stupid and people who had biases were ignorant. I knew that there was a wide world out there and many different peoples were living there. I knew that the Japanese, who were so proud in their own country, were not well respected in other parts of the world. I was sorry that I was too young and unable to present the argument logically. Even if I could, no Japanese person would have believed me. In those days, the Japanese believed they were the superior race and the Koreans and the Chinese were inferior. My mother was painfully conscious of the prejudice against Koreans. I think she was hurt because she was forever foreign to Koreans. It hurt even more when people tended to think that any Japanese woman who would marry a Korean must have come from dubious origins.

She was disowned by her step-father. Her step-father could not believe that a poor Korean young man would marry his daughter for nothing. Surely, he was marrying her for the money she would inherit. Nothing was further from the truth. I feel deep sadness when I think of it. Prior to my father, my step-grandfather married my mother to a Japanese man who he thought would not steal or squander his money, but it did not work out. My mother had a baby girl who lived only a short while as if she had no desire to live in a family where there was no love. I think of her from time to time. I don't even know her name. I am sorry I did not ask my mother while she was still alive.

In olden days when women did not receive much education, the death of a husband immediately meant financial difficulties. One method of earning money was to board students. A woman who was renting one of the houses that belonged to my step-grandfather was doing exactly that. One of the students happened to be a Korean. One day, when my mother went to this house to collect the rent, my father was visiting him. A pair of large shoes was lying at the door. "My, what big feet," was her impression. My father was tall and handsome. My mother was not particularly hampered by stereo-typical Japanese customs. So my father took my mother to Chinatown in Yokohama (the Chinatown in Yokohama was big and thriving) and introduced her to yet another foreign element.

This was the first time my mother tasted some Chinese foods although I don't think she appreciated them much. Her palate was Japanese whereas my father's taste was closer to that of the Chinese. Koreans are meat-eating people and they are born with a stomach that demands food every hour. The tiny delicate Japanese portions would never have satisfied my father's or my stomach. Among the many Korean traits I inherited, I also got the appetite. It was a well-known fact that the Japanese appreciated the plate rather than the food on it. Koreans would have given that portion to a canary.

Soon, two young people plunged into marriage without knowing what it would involve. Ignorance was their ally. They could not afford a marriage ceremony so they went to Meiji shrine and bowed in front of the altar and got married legally. Her step-father asked her whether she would change her mind or not and, when he found out that she would not, he brought her all the kimonos he had bought for her and told her that this would be the last time he would see her. She was cut off from the family and the relatives who belonged to the clan.

While we were living in this house, my mother took us often to Yamashita Park. It was named after Yamashita Shipping Lines, one of the largest shipping companies in Japan. The park was located right next to the pier. Big white ships were docked at the piers. The beautiful elegant curves of their sterns reminded me of big white swans. The ships stirred in me an unknown nostalgia for exotic lands. My sister and I played on the swings. When I swung the swing high up into the air, I felt I was going to land on one of the white ships that was resting in the water. My mother's kimono sleeves were swaying in the breeze. She was wearing a silk kimono of the "yagasuri" (pattern of arrows) design. The arrows were black against the brownish brick colour of the kimono. This kimono was later converted into the cover of a comforter. Turning an old kimono into the cover of a comforter was a common practice. My mother was trying to hold her hair in place with one hand. She was looking out to the sea with a far-away look and I could tell that she was woman and not just a mother.

In order to get to Yamashita Park, we took commuter trains. In Japan, the public transit system had already been well developed. To get to a platform, we had to go up flights of stairs. On the landing there often stood an automatic vending machine. For five sen, the machine would spit out a small-sized chocolate or a small-sized packet of caramel candies. For ten sen, we would get bigger sizes. Inside the ten-sen chocolate wrapping lay a coloured photo of an American female movie star and the candy box had a little toy stuck on the top of the box. It was something similar to the little toys one gets in cereal boxes here. The chocolate was wrapped in silver paper which we rolled into a ball and waited for it to grow in size. There were two famous confectionery companies, Meiji and Morinaga. I preferred the taste of Morinaga to that of Meiji. Ten sen, in those days, was not an amount of money to be taken lightly, so it was not always that I got a bigger bar of chocolate but when I did, I carefully put away the picture of the star. I thought they were the most beautiful women.

Traveling on public transportation caused us some unpleasantness. When I was four, we were stopped at the entrance of a railway station by an employee who punched the tickets. All public transit was free for children under six. Since I was half Korean and inherited the genes of a tall person, I was always very tall for my age. The railway employee did not believe that I was only four. My mother tried in vain to explain to him that I was not six and we were not trying to cheat. In order to truly convince him, she would have to disclose the fact that I was half Korean. So in the end, she reluctantly gave in and paid the fare. The fact that we had a Korean surname was a secret we guarded carefully.

One of my childhood memories is of my mother putting on make-up in the morning. I loved to watch the ritual of a grown woman transforming herself. For her eyebrows, my mother burnt an ordinary bottle cork and used the soot. Her hair had to be ironed everyday. At first she placed a curling iron on a gas range to heat it up. When she thought it was hot enough, she would test it on a piece of newspaper. Sometimes it was over-heated; the paper turned brown and I could smell it burning.

Her cosmetics consisted of vanishing cream, Coty face powder and Three Flowers rouge. Coty in those days was the epitome of high fashion and so was Three Flowers. Coty was French and Three Flowers was American. Coty has now disappeared from the market and Three Flowers had not been seen for years. Three Flowers did not come back onto the Japanese market even after World War II and I used to wonder what happened to it. Later, I found it in a show window of a drug store in Germany. The trade mark was of a lady making up her face and another woman standing behind her. A gush of childhood memory came back to me. Apparently, a German company bought it but they kept the English name.

My mother was a charming nice-looking woman. In the days when no decent nice-looking Japanese woman would sink so low as to marry a Korean, an inferior human being, my mother was a surprise. Their marriage was actually so sensational that a reputable Japanese newspaper reported it. It was the second Korean-Japanese mixed marriage after the annexation of Korea. The first one was that between Prince Lee and Princess Nashimoto.

People were always curious to know why we looked nice and decent because the Japanese could not believe that Koreans could also look nice and decent if they were given the opportunity. It did not occur to them that the reason why Koreans were poor and were not in positions of power was due to the Japanese oppression of Korea. My father's colleagues at the company were very curious about his wife. They wanted to know what kind of Japanese woman he had married. My father had a mischievous spirit and was an expert in cracking jokes. He told his female co-workers that his wife had buck teeth, was cross-eyed and generally ugly. In those days working women were despised for not being rich enough to stay home and be idle. They worked hard for little money and little fun. One of them decided to have a good laugh at this Korean's ugly wife. One Sunday, she decked herself out in her best kimono, made of cheap man-made material, and came to visit my family. She was greeted by a pretty young wife who was clad in a kimono, more expensive than hers, and two lovely children. She went home livid. She never spoke to him again at the office. Later my mother scolded my father for upsetting the poor girl unnecessarily.

My father was tall and good looking. He kept his dignified looks until the last moment of his life. In the days when the Japanese were small, everything was made to fit their size and, was therefore too small for him. He had to be careful not to bang his forehead against the doorsill. The sleeves of jackets were too short and his shoes were big. Temperamentally, he did not worry about small matters like the Japanese and often rubbed them the wrong way. He was not meek like the Japanese. His temper would flare up at any insult to his pride as a Korean, but when he was in a good mood, he was a nice father to us. I loved my father and got along well with him because he was intelligent and educated. Unlike other feudalistic Oriental men, he was open to women's education. Since he was a man of few words, my sister was rather afraid of him. I, too, was afraid of arousing his anger knowing his explosive temper. But he did not mind playing with his children. One of the games he willingly played with me was to let me stand on his big feet, hold his hands and walk around the room. I was riding on his feet instead of on his back.

While the majority of the Japanese discriminated against Koreans, my parents did have some Japanese friends. Like leaves blown into a corner, these friends were also carrying a social stigma. The wife of one couple was a nurse. She was working in Formosa and fell in love with a patient, a big taboo for his family. The family did not allow them to marry so they eloped. The husband was suffering from tuberculosis and was almost in the last stage of the disease. Since they had eloped to Japan, they had no means of supporting themselves and were struggling to keep their heads above water. Tuberculosis in those days was equivalent to a death sentence. The only cure was a natural method but most patients got impatient and desperate and died just from the despair.

The other couple belonged to the "Etta" class. Although the new Meiji government abolished this class legally, the social stigma had not disappeared. This class was similar to the caste of "Untouchables" in India. Prior to the new government's regulations, the people who belonged to this class were ex-convicts, social outcasts, the people who were born there by fate and those who treated animal skins. The Japanese had not eaten the meat of beasts before the Meiji period and therefore regarded the people who had anything to do with beasts with great contempt and suspicion. The Etta class lived in huts under the bridge in Kyoto and were not allowed to interact with ordinary citizens. There were quite a few sad love stories between a citizen of the Etta class and that of the ordinary class. After the restoration in 1868, this abominable class was abolished and the people of Etta lived in a village near Kyoto, but the social stigma remained. Others could tell at once when they heard their surname. Not many families would accept one from the Etta class. This couple escaped to the Tokyo-Yokohama area where people did not know much about Etta surnames. They always lived in fear that someday someone might find out. Like us Koreans, they avoided, as much as possible, the occasions where they had to mention their name.

One evening these friends came to visit us. It must have been a summer day. I still remember my father waving a Japanese fan back and forth trying to cool himself. In Japanese families, children were always included. They did not seclude themselves in separate rooms with a door. The Japanese houses with sliding doors were open spaces. Children stayed around grown-ups, listening to their conversations, thus acquiring knowledge about life through the ear. It is called "mimi gakumon" (knowledge gained by listening). Occasionally, adults would say: "This is not for children. Go somewhere else." Then we went away, dying of curiosity. Otherwise, we would calmly listen to a woman pouring out her personal problems to another woman. On the evening of their visit, my sister and I were playing near the grown-ups. I was wearing one of my mother's petticoats. She owned two of these. One of them was plain white cotton with just a little bit of lace but the other, more expensive one, was daintily decorated with a lot of eyelets. This petticoat looked to me so beautiful and exquisite. It was not always that she would let me wear this one. But this evening I had the privilege of wearing it. Since I was small and the petticoat long, it was like an evening gown. I felt gorgeous and pretended to be a queen. But after a while of vigorous playing, the queen became sleepy. My parents laid out an underfuton beside them so I could lie down and go to sleep while my ear was still listening to the gossip. My mother brought out a thin cover but did not cover me right away, obviously thinking it would be too hot. The night was getting cooler and I wanted to use the cover but I somehow wanted to test the depth of my mother's love. How soon would she notice that I needed to be covered? I closed my eyes tightly, pretending to be asleep. Time passed and I really wanted the cover but I did not try to cover myself. It had to be my mother who would notice it. Some more time passed and I felt my mother's gentle hand placing the cover over me. I fell asleep with a feeling of satisfaction.

It was during this time that I learned the word "baka" (stupid). The children in the neighbourhood were throwing this derogatory word at one another. My mother wanted to bring up her children properly so she forbade us to use such a word. My elder sister, who inherited more Japanese blood that I did, obediently nodded. One day, while my mother was washing clothes, she heard someone calling out: "Baka, Baka, Bakayaro." She stopped washing and came out to the gate because it sounded awfully close to her house. To her horror, it was I who was shouting the vulgar words to the Japanese children. Standing beside me was my elder sister, meekly repeating our mother's instruction: "You mustn't say 'baka', you mustn't say 'baka'."

One day, suddenly, I lost my playmate. Since some neighbours did not want their children to play with Korean children, my sister and I kept each other company all the time. But she was no longer there during the daytime. She had started school. She left home early in the morning in a blue sailor dress with a folded white handkerchief pinned on her breast with a safety pin. My memory is now blurred and I am not sure whether one's name was written by brush and India ink on the handkerchief or on a little round piece of cardboard. At any rate, this was for the teacher to learn the children's names and after a while they did not have to wear them. There were usually four classes to each year with each class consisting of 50 to 60 children. I stayed home and played by myself but it was not the same as playing with my sister. One day I lost patience. I got on a stool with a ladle in my hand. I was pretending that I was speaking on the phone. In those days, a telephone was installed on the wall and the receiver was tube-shaped. "Ring, ring, moshimoshi, is that school?" I spoke into the ladle, "please, send my sister back quickly. I am lonely."

My sister had a special talent for causing more headaches and anxiety for my mother than I did. As a baby she had colic and screamed at night for two years. Her crying would start at the first sound of the noodle vendor's horn and would go on for two hours. For some unknown reason, she suddenly stopped this practice after two years. One of the curious neighbours asked my mother: "Is your daughter gone?" In comparison, I was an easy baby. I did not cry often and knew how to occupy myself alone. Later, my sister could not cope well with people who insulted her for being half Korean. She never could fight back. She also often managed to pick up problematic diseases. As soon as she started school, she picked up a skin disease called "shitsu" for which there was no known cure.

In Japanese schools, children changed outside shoes into sneakers to walk around the school. The sneakers were left at school. To store the sneakers, there were shoe lockers at the entrance of the school. Although the shoe lockers had no locks, theft was rare. Public schools had pupils from all kinds of families and a lot of them came from families who ran small shops and of working class. These parents were too busy to worry about the well-being of their children. One of the children, who came from such a family, had this skin disease and had her shoe locker next to my sister's. Out of 50 children or so, my sister was the only one who contracted it and she was the only one who diligently washed her hands at every recess. My mother kept the house spic and span and we children were always clean and well dressed. Science preaches to us that keeping ourselves clean and washed prevents us from getting germs. My sister's situation proved the opposite.

Later, I acquired a philosophy of my own. If you don't want to get sick, don't worry about it. Keep yourself reasonably unhygienic. Don't wash your hands constantly. Keep some germs on yourself so that you can build up some immunity. Your time of birth and death is in God's hands. When you are destined to live, you shall live under all circumstances. Human efforts cannot prolong your life.

My sister, I am sure, contracted this skin disease because she washed her hands too often; her cleanliness offered an ideal vacuum for the germs to multiply. No medication worked. There was no known cure for it actually. Her hands were covered by white bandages which my mother changed conscientiously, but blood seeped through the bandages as if to show us the gravity of the disease. My mother forbade us to hold hands with her. She also frantically tried every type of medication. Nothing worked. Finally she invented her own recipe and tried it. She chased me out to the garden and instructed me not to come back in until she called me. She closed all the doors and burned highly toxic sulphur in a "kotatsu".

Kotatsu is an ineffective traditional Japanese device to warm oneself. One places a square three dimensional wooden frame in the room and covers it with a comforter. Within the frame, one places a brazier with ashes and charcoal. A family sits around this kotatsu, puts their feet, legs and hands under the cover and warms themselves. This method of heating keeps one's feet and legs warm up to a certain point but keeps one's shoulders and back cold. Consequently, once one sits down to a kotatsu, one does not want to take out one's limbs and get up. In olden days when the elderly and males were the authorities, they would order children and females to go and get something while they stayed in the sanctuary of the kotatsu. Sometimes they would place a small table on top of the covered wooden frame to play cards or to have a place to put teacups or mandarin oranges. Sometimes lovers held hands under the kotatsu while they kept cool faces above it.

My mother burnt sulphur in a brazier, risking the danger of toxic fumes and my sister put her hands under the cover. After a few tense moments, she opened up all the screen doors and fanned out the smell of sulphur. This drastic method worked and my sister's hands were cured of the disease.

Our relatively peaceful stable life in this house was to end very soon. One day, a green snake crawled out of our garden. In those days, cities, even large cities like Tokyo, had areas that offered a habitat for snakes. The house we lived in was in the suburbs where there were bushes, trees and wild plants. In such surroundings, very often, snakes nested under the houses or in the spaces between the roofs and ceilings. Usually they were harmless green snakes. They can grow quite long and wide. My memory tells me that this one was about nine centimetres wide and one metre long. Now, in Japan, there are many wise sayings that have been handed down from generation to generation. One of them is: "Never kill snakes; if you do, you will be cursed." My father was young, reckless and scoffed at superstition. He killed it and threw it into the nearby stream. A few days later, another snake appeared. I think they were mates, and after one was killed, its mate came out looking for it. My father killed this one and threw it into the stream, too. While grown-ups were running around, I stood in the garden, trembling. Something green moved in front of me and I started thinking: "What shall I do, if this turns into a snake?" I admired my father. He was strong. I felt secure and protected because he was there.

Shortly after this incident, my father decided to quit his stable job and take his family to Korea in search of gold, as if the curse of the snakes clouded his wisdom.

chapter II

The sea was brownish and the sky hung heavily in a grim grey, as if to foretell our future in Korea. To cross over to Korea from Japan, we had to take a train from Tokyo to Shimonoseki, which is situated at the southern part of Honshu Island (Main Island), and then take an eight-hour-long ferry ride. The inside of the ferry was like a big dormitory without chairs. One had to secure a space on the floor. The atmosphere was crammed and oppressive, so I escaped to the deck to watch the waves. No one was around on the deck because everyone, including my family, was seasick. The waves were high and rough. The little ship went up and down like a swing that had lost one side of the string. I was enjoying the sense of danger. Every time the waves billowed, as if to engulf the little ship and crush it into the white foam, the ship rose and sank rhythmically.

The strait between Japan and Korea is the only sea that is known to have sharks. All around Japan, even the sea known for its roughness, has no sharks. Did Korea want to prevent invaders from coming by inviting the sharks? It was said that if a woman was thrown into the sea by accident, she should untie the "obi" (a sash a Japanese woman wears on her kimono) so that she would be longer that the length of a shark, as a shark will not attack anything longer than itself. The rails that separated me from the deep sea had big spaces between the bars. With a sudden jerk of the ship, I could have easily fallen into the sea. In those days, grown-ups did not rush around to protect and support their children. With more than one child in a family, no washing machine, dryer and other gadgets to help the housewife, everyone, even children, had to be independent and responsible. Children looked after themselves without constant supervision from adults.

My memories are choppy. My next clear recollection is about my father's native village, situated in a very northern part of Korea, close to the Yalu River. The river was the boundary line between Korea and Manchuria. Hence, my father had looked very similar to Manchurians. The river often froze in severe winters, thus making the invasion from China easy. China coveted the area where ginseng grew and invaded Korea several times, trying to take possession of the land. The effectiveness of ginseng does not lie in the plant but in the soil. The plant must grow in that area to have its magical healing power. To everyone's surprise, though, little Korea repelled their powerful neighbor successfully.

The influence of China was more evident in Korea than in Japan. My father's so-called house consisted of separate living quarters scattered around in a big compound where the extended family lived together. A Korean family consisted of grandparents (if alive), parents, children, cousins, aunts, uncles, any other relative who required help and a guest who happened to pass by and had a whim to stay on. Thus, Koreans could never keep their wealth for any length of time because of their excessive hospitality. All the responsibility of looking after this large family fell upon the shoulder of the man of the house and when the father died, it was passed onto the eldest son. The eldest son of a Korean family was treated differently from the rest of the family. He was treated like a king. Even his clothing and food were different. My father who was the eldest son of this family was supposed to be performing this duty but he escaped this heavy burden, which would have hampered his ambition to better himself, by marrying a foreign woman. His next oldest brother was looking after the family. My uncle was an honest, trustworthy man of integrity.

When we arrived in this village, it was late spring. I saw women clad in traditional Korean costumes milling around, cooking, cleaning and washing. Their cooking stove was the traditional outdoor charcoal burner. I don't know from where the money to support this large family came. My great-grandfather, who owned acres of land and was very wealthy, spent it all like a stream of water and by the time my grandfather came along, the family was not well off. The Japanese invasion did not make the situation any better. On the whole, almost all Koreans were poor except a few who cooperated with the Japanese. The arrival of my mother in a kimono caused a great sensation. My mother told us later that she was like a movie star. Nobody in this remote village had seen a live Japanese woman in such strange attire. Everywhere she went, children, who were my relations in some way, followed her in groups, dying of curiosity.

The family allotted us living quarters in their compound. The room facing the open area had screen doors. The weather was already getting warm. My mother, who was used to healthy airy Japanese houses, could not stand sleeping with the doors closed. Korean houses are not made to let too much air in because they have to shut out every breath of cold air during the harsh winter. So she left the doors open during the night. Next morning, when my uncle came to bid us "Good Morning", he was stunned to see the wide-open doors.

"Sister," he said, "you didn't leave these doors open, did you?"

"Yes, we did," she answered innocently.

His eyes grew wide. He congratulated us for not having become a dinner for a tiger. (I wonder why my father did not worry. Maybe he had forgotten during his long absence from his native land.) Tigers were not extinct in Korea then. They came visiting villages often. Korean folklore often treats tigers as subjects of the stories.

Now, it is not only adults who suffer from culture shock. Strange surroundings upset me as well as my mother. I did not know that the woman in a beige traditional Korean costume was my own grandmother. When she tried to hold me, her own son's daughter, I flinched. She had tears in her eyes. Now I have tears in my eyes when I think of it. I am sorry, Grandmother!

As I said before, my memories are sketchy. In my next vivid memory, I was running after my mother in the yard. I had just recovered from an illness. I was very ill with dysentery and had been in a hospital for many days. The change in the diet and water was the cause of the illness. Koreans use a lot of garlic and red pepper in their foods. My father's family knew that we, who came from Japan, could not tolerate garlic, so they separated our portion of food from theirs and did not put any garlic in ours. But the smell of garlic is so strong that it stuck to the kitchen utensils, cooking pots and crockery. So, instead of eating proper meals, I stuffed myself with corn and drank the water I was not used to. I came down with a very bad case of dysentery.

I remember lying in bed. Occasionally I opened my eyes. The surroundings were grey and I heard loud adults' voices. I was in a deep coma and the voices I heard when I came back to the surface of consciousness were those of the relatives who came to visit the sick. Koreans have a deep sense of community. Any incident and the whole clan would gather round. Everything was the opposite of what my mother was used to. When she saw no sign of improvement in me, she insisted that I should be moved to a modern hospital, run by American missionaries. Many opposed her opinion, saying that moving such a sick child would kill it. But finally my mother won. I was wrapped up in a comforter and transported to the hospital. My elder sister's illness was milder than mine. She was a cautious eater and never at any time gulped down a huge quantity of food, as I did. So she recovered easily and stayed home.

My father brought his family to Korea because he believed the word of one of his uncles that they would find gold and strike it rich. In retrospect, I think my father was like me or I like him. I could never work from 9 to 5 and deal with complicated human relations. In order to earn a living, my father had to work in a Japanese company with people of a different national temperament and put up with constant racial prejudice. I couldn't blame him for wanting to quit and go his own way. The best occupation that would have suited him was law. He had excellent legal knowledge and a lawyer's erratic schedule would have suited him. But he was barred from doing what he most liked because he was Korean. Japanese did not give licenses to Koreans to practice law. He uprooted his family for speculation. The mountain that was supposed to contain gold, stood there cold and realistic, crushing his hopes. How he paid the hospital expenses, I do not know.

My grandmother, who did not receive much formal education, was an intelligent and sensitive woman. During my illness, she went everyday to a shrine nearby to pray for my recovery. Apparently, she said explicitly: "My daughter-in-law would not have come all the way from Japan to a remote village like this for the love of my son. She came for the love of their children. If that child dies here, she will haunt me all through her life."

My mother told us later that though her family and my father's family were of different nationalities and lived far apart from each other, there were many similarities in their philosophy of life, ways of thinking and manners. My grandmother's sensitivity was an example. My uncle, next in line to my father, despite his poverty, would change his clothes and take a present whenever he went visiting. He kept the family going despite the fact that it was not his duty and was always kind and considerate to us. My poor grandmother!

She lost her eldest son to a foreign woman and her grandchildren were strangers to her. My mother's parents lost their child to a foreigner and thus two families lost their loved ones.

I miraculously recovered and I could run in the yard after my mother.

Besides the foods that smelt of garlic, the privy was a horror to us. It was outside in a sort of big hut. Inside, there was a big hole and two planks of wood were placed over it like a bridge. I was only five years old so the hole seemed to me like a gaping abyss and the human soils that filled the hole were enough to make me want to throw up.

Shortly after I recovered, we left the village to go to Seoul. We had had enough of village life. On the day of departure, all the relatives came to say good-bye. My sister and I were each presented with a little red beaded handbag with a silver chain. My sister's was a little more elaborate than mine because she was older. In each handbag there was a five-yen bill, which was a lot of money in those days. The money was taken away by our parents and was used for housekeeping. When my sister and I grew up, we jokingly reminded them, from time to time, of the money.

My father must have gone ahead to Seoul to prepare for our arrival. It must have been my uncle who put us on the train. My mother, who had never traveled alone before, was nervous. Her knowledge of Korean was limited to one phrase, "Where is a toilet?" She was always clad in a kimono and people could not tell from the outside that she was a Korean's wife. We, the children, did not exactly fall into the category of typical Korean children. Since there was a strong anti-Japanese feeling in Korea, looking so Japanese was not a very good idea.

There was a Japanese fellow sitting nearby. He must have sensed my mother's nervousness. He spoke to her kindly and struck up a conversation. He asked her where we were going, which suitcases we had to carry and other usual questions. At the end he assured my mother that he would help us carry the suitcases. When the train pulled in the station of Seoul, he grabbed the suitcases. My innocent mother thanked him profusely. However, after a few minutes she realized what his true intention was. He started walking very fast to distance himself from the naive woman who was encumbered by two young children. My mother accelerated her pace, too. Although she was a short woman and wore a kimono, which was inconvenient attire for running, she ran, almost dragging us by both hands. When the man got to the exit, we were right behind him. He put the suitcases down on the ground and my mother thanked him again. She was truly grateful because she did not have to carry the suitcases!

The city of Seoul was much smaller than Tokyo and looked dilapidated. It seemed to have sunk in a grey stupor and nothing was actively moving since it was the Japanese policy to keep Korea oppressed. But life somehow survived.

We rented a house in the Japanese section of the city that was on the top of the hill. At the bottom of the hill lived Koreans and Chinese. There was a small Chinatown in the middle of the Korean community. A lot of Japanese who went to Korea were losers in their own society. Anybody who could not find a job in Japan could land a job in Korea for the simple reason that he was Japanese. In short, they were not nice people and had very strong prejudices against Koreans. But fortunately, there was one Japanese family in the neighborhood who had no prejudice against us. They had a son about our age, called Masao. He and I played together. But there was another family whose husband was a Japanese civil servant. I could tell even as a child that the wife was a fake and she was trying to keep up appearances. She probably did not like her only daughter, Hiroko, playing with Korean-mixed children but she could not help it because Masao and we were the only other children in the neighborhood. My sixth sense told me that this family did not have much money. A Japanese civil servant's salary was not much. Their pretension to look better than us made them hypocrites. Their way of living was reflected in their daughter and she was not a very pleasant person.

One day, Hiroko came over to our house. One of the natural products Korea produced and Japan did not, was a kind of honey melon. It was juicy and very tasty. We did not have much money but my mother never skimped on food. So she often bought the melon and served us liberally. When Hiroko came over, my mother brought out a tray full of melon slices. Since she was the guest, my mother offered them to her first.

"Take one," she said. Hiroko's eyes scanned the melon slices eagerly and greedily and her fingers picked up the largest slice. "Wow," I said to myself, "here's a Japanese girl who despises Koreans and yet she picks up the largest slice of melon from the Korean plate."

Since the Japanese community was on the top of the hill and the shops were some distance away, a Chinese green grocery vendor came to sell vegetables from his peddling cart. When he arrived, he would ring a bell and all the wives would come out and do their shopping. Inevitably the civil servant's wife would bargain and bargain. One morning, my mother heard a soft knock at the front door. When she went to check who the visitor was, the Chinese green grocer was standing there. "Madam," he said, "come quickly and do your shopping. When Mrs._____ (civil servant's wife) comes, I am going to raise the prices." After my mother had bought everything she needed, the grocer rang the bell and settled down to bargain leisurely.

One day in June, my elder sister and I were told to go outside and play. After a while, a woman in a white apron came out of the house and beckoned us to come in. When we went in, we saw our mother lying in bed with a tiny baby beside her. In olden days, women usually produced their babies at home with the help of a midwife. The woman in the white apron was the midwife. I did not know that a baby could descend upon us so suddenly. But when I saw the little bundle, I felt love for my newborn sister. I rushed out again announcing loudly to the world that we had a new baby.

Shortly after the birth of my sister, my mother took ill. By then, my father's youngest sister, Injo, had come to live with us. She, like my father, wanted to study and better herself. The family did not have enough means to send her to Seoul to study. They could not afford it for a son, let alone for a daughter. My father was the only one in the family who managed to get out of the village and get a higher education. Now they hoped that he could help her to get some education. At the time we were poor. My father could not send her to a proper five-year girl's school (joggakko). So she enrolled herself in a four-year commercial school. Even then she was overjoyed. I still remember her happily going to school everyday in a uniform, carrying an embroidery frame. She was already nineteen according to the Oriental calculation, the age when other joggakko students graduate. She was actually seventeen according to the western way of calculation.

When my mother became ill, Injo was the oldest female in the household. Naturally, all the household duties, including looking after the newborn baby, fell upon her shoulders. When she had to change the baby's diapers, she cried. Her family may have been poor but she was shielded from performing such lowly duties as dealing with human soils. She was too young to keep a house with three young children. She came to Seoul to study and not to look after a household with a sick woman and her children. She did her best—the best a seventeen-year-old could, but the place got dirty and was not up to the standard my mother wished. My mother was Japanese and kept the children and the house spic and span. When she saw the condition of the kitchen and flies flying about, she shuddered. (I think her sensitivity made her vulnerable to the disease.)

My father was away in search of work. My mother was anxiously awaiting his return to solve the problem of this unhygienic state. She soon suspected that she must have caught typhus. A fever that went up and down in a pattern and persistent perspiration were some of the symptoms of this disease. In those days, average households had no flush toilet. The night soils were collected periodically by the people who later sold it to the farmers. It was one of the occupations held by many Koreans because they were barred by the Japanese from white-collar jobs. Flies were the result of this type of toilet and germs were transmitted by them. My mother was generally nervous about germs. When she saw the flies dancing around the kitchen as a result of Injo's sloppy housekeeping, she had already caught the disease in her mind. Added to her physical weakness after childbirth, she actually became very, very ill. Since my father was away, she just lay in bed and whenever she used the toilet, she poured disinfectant in the toilet bowl and disinfected everything she touched.

My father finally came home and a doctor was called. The doctor pronounced that she had typhoid, not typhus. The former is a worse disease than the latter. Since it was contagious, she had to be quarantined. An ambulance came to pick her up and my father carried her out. With her hair hanging about and her pallid complexion, she did not even look like my mother. I stood there and watched her being carried out without any particular emotion. She looked like a stranger. The neighbors came out to watch this spectacle half curiously and half sympathetically. They also wished that they would not catch it. The house had to be fumigated. I was happily jumping around as two men from the city went around the house with the equipment. White powder covered the rooms.

The household without its mother nearly collapsed. The most pressing matter was the feeding of a forty-day-old baby. I remember my father standing at the cooking stove in the kitchen, stirring a pot with one hand while holding my sister with the other hand. He didn't know how to hold a baby properly so he simply held her close to his body with one arm. Half of the baby was hanging down from his arm. But my sister did not object to it. She got so used to this strange way of holding that she cried when my mother came home and held her in the proper motherly way. I can't remember what my father and Injo were feeding us but I remember distinctly that baby's clothes were always white and clean and I was never hungry.

I can't say that our appearance was all right. After a while when my mother had recovered enough to receive visitors, my father took us to see her at the hospital and my mother gasped at the sight of us. Our bangs were down to our eyebrows, (it wasn't fashionable then; it meant only one thing: you couldn't afford a hairdresser) because my father was too busy to think of sending us to a barber (we children went to a barber, not to a hairdresser), our dresses hung from our bodies like tired seaweed and we were wearing sneakers without socks. (This was in the 1930s. We would have fitted in comfortably in the crowds on the streets in the 1990s.) As much as my mother was surprised, I was shocked at the sight of her. Her face was no longer deathly but she was wearing an old kimono, her face had no make-up and her hair just hung like a dirty mop.

When my mother was brought to the hospital, she was in a coma. She told us later that when one got to that stage, one could hear what others were saying but could not speak. Her voice was gone. In those days, even now in certain cases, any patient had to hire a hospital aid or a member of the family had to stay at the bedside to look after the patient. My mother was assigned a Japanese woman, a battered-by-life, hardened and tough woman. My mother heard her say out loud (because she thought my mother could not hear): "I am sure these stingy Koreans won't give me a sen for a tip." The next time my father went to see her and she had recovered the ability to talk, she told him what she had heard. He tipped the woman handsomely. The woman's attitude changed instantly like the flip of a hand. At mealtimes, she rushed to the front of the line-up in the kitchen and grabbed the biggest piece of watermelon. She changed the sheets of the bed efficiently and carried the bed pan willingly. She took care of my mother well and helped her recover. This, however, was a sad confirmation of the statement: "Money buys even the gate-keeper of hell."

At home my father struggled on with the help of a housekeeper. He desperately needed someone to wash the baby's diapers, the washing of which was done by hand with a scrub board and a tub. The first woman who came was Japanese. She came in a traditional kimono, sat in the Japanese way (legs folded under her), placed her "kappogi"(Japanese apron that covers the whole front) beside her, bowed and spoke in polite Japanese. I sensed at once that she was a fake. I could tell even as a child that she had been battered in life and was not as kind as she tried to sound. Life must have been treating her badly. Why else would she come to Seoul, leaving her own country to work for a Korean family? She did not come back after a few days. Maybe my father had no money and fell behind in the payments.

Next, came a motherly Korean woman who did not speak a word of Japanese. She was the opposite of the Japanese woman who had just left. She came in a traditional Korean outfit and sat in the Korean manner (with one knee up). Like all other Korean women she was casual, did not worry about small details, did not rush around but spent more time sitting and smiling at us benevolently. She must have felt at home since the head of the family was of the same blood and the children had no prejudice. I liked her. She may not have been too much of a help to my father but she was warm and kind. In olden days, the majority of Japanese families used old summer kimonos as diapers. They would cut up the kimono into diaper-sized pieces.

My mother, who was gradually influenced by my father, admired and loved the American way and abhorred the Japanese custom, so she bought American white diapers made of gauzy material. But these diapers had to be folded in a certain manner after a wash. After she had washed them, the "omoni" (means mother in Korean) sat smiling because she did not know how to fold them. She had never seen American diapers before. My elder sister did not talk to strangers easily. So I took it upon myself to instruct the "omoni" how to fold the diapers. I sat next to her, spread out the white material and went step by step, all the while speaking in pidgin Japanese as if she would understand the language if I spoke in broken Japanese. The "omoni" obviously understood my intention. She took one diaper out of the pile and followed the movement of my hands. "There," I said benevolently, "that's very good." Then we beamed at each other. I don't think she was doing too much work. All I can remember vividly is her sitting in a white "chogori" (blouse) and "chima" (skirt) with one knee up, just smiling. I can't remember eating what she might have cooked.

With no parental supervision, I spent a lot of time in the park nearby. There were swings and a slide in the park. With my bangs hanging down over my eyebrows and looking like a waif, I slid down the slide over and over again. I did not notice that there was a huge nail sticking out from the side of the slide. I was sliding down happily and vigorously and then it caught me. It tore away a chunk of flesh from my left knee. I ran back home with blood dripping. In those days, the first aid for open wounds was to sterilize it with oxidole (called oxiful in Japanese). Injo felt faint when she saw the wound. The poor thing summoned all her courage and tried to clean it. But every time she attempted, I cringed and wailed. So she just patted it with a cotton ball. This perfunctory treatment led to the infection of the wound and pus and blood kept oozing out from the wound. It remained in that condition until my mother came home. One of her first tasks to tackle upon her return was to clean the wound thoroughly and put proper ointment on it. The wound healed quickly but it left a permanent scar on my knee.

My mother stayed at the hospital for forty days and my father took my elder sister and me to visit her. As we walked down the hallway to get to my mother's room, I glimpsed the rooms packed with patients who came for free treatment. In Korea, almost everyone was poor due to the Japanese oppression. A lot of Koreans could not eat properly, which caused skin diseases. The desperate air, that hung over the whole of Korea, was bad enough outside but, inside the dark rooms, it was almost unbearable. I turned my eyes away but the image of the patients was already etched on my inner mind and my heart ached with sympathy. When we got to her room, she was sitting up in her bed. There were three other women in her room in various stages of recovery. My mother still looked like a stranger to me. She smiled at us but I felt uneasy. Her hair was hanging down loose and her summer kimono was not put on properly. I wanted my pretty mother back.

My mother, who everyone thought would die, recovered. The young Japanese woman in the next bed died. She was a schoolteacher who went on a holiday to the Continent and contracted typhus on the way home. It was fashionable in those days for Japanese to go to the Continent (Korea, Manchuria and northern China) for holidays. But they did not understand that the Continent was not an extension of Japan just because the Japanese occupied those areas. The Japanese who were used to Japan's mild climate had no idea that the Continent's climate was harsher, epidemics were more violent and the concept of hygiene was different. She took ill when she got to Korea and died alone in a strange country. One never knows what fate has in its mind. On the day my mother was released from the hospital, all the staff came to the front door to say good-bye to her. They had never thought that she would walk out of that door alive.

As soon as she came home, she had to tackle various tasks that had piled up. The number one priority was to feed my sister, Keiko, and fatten her up. She was alive and well but was very thin. My father's best efforts could not measure up to a mother's efficiency. My mother trotted off to the American missionary hospital nearby to get the most nutritious formula for the baby because she could no longer feed her herself. It must have been a Catholic hospital. My mother talked often about a serene-looking Korean nun who later came to visit us to see how the baby was doing. The Christian American formula worked well on my sister. Within a week, her wrist had a double fold. All the women in the neighborhood admired the merits of a mother.

While I was in Korea, I started school. According to the Oriental calculation, everyone became a year older on New Year's Day, regardless of when one was born during the year. A baby who was born on December 31 became two years old on the next day. All the children who were born between April and December and were eight years old on New Year's Day and all the children who were born between January and March and were seven years old on New Year's Day, entered school at the same time. My elder sister had already begun school in Japan so she was transferred to a Korean private school. The Japanese school in Seoul did not accept her because she was a Korean national by birth. The school was the most posh private school in Seoul and the children, who were attending it, came from families much wealthier than ours. The Japanese government needed some collaboration from the Koreans so it sought the help of some prestigious Korean families who were willing to cooperate. As long as they cooperated, they could earn a living. The majority of them worked with the Japanese out of necessity. Our family was poor so my parents could not afford a uniform for my sister. She went to school in the old sailor dress she wore in Japan.

I entered the same school in April. Because my sister was the pioneer, I had no difficulty in passing the entrance examination. This became a pattern. Later, when I entered Keisen Girls School, it was her presence at the school that let me get in without a hassle. My poor elder sister, who was diligent but never made the top ten of the class, had to make a track which I just followed. At school, I was a crybaby. I hated being away from home. My dislike for a pack life was already obvious. Since my mother had spoiled me before the birth of my younger sister, I was uncoordinated physically and emotionally. I cried once a day like a ritual. So once a day, someone had to go to my sister and tell her: "Your sister is crying again." My sister did not know what to do but for me, the sight of a family member was enough. My father was worried since I seemed to be having so much difficulty adjusting to school. He came often to school to check how I was coping. Once he came during a gym class.

Despite the fact that I was always the tallest girl in class, I was also the slowest girl in running. While my father was standing watching, it became my turn to run. As I was running, I noticed my father. I turned my head to look at him. He half laughed and waved his hand to signal me to go on and not look back. I can still see him in my mind, my father, young and handsome and I want to cry.

The teachers were all Korean. My mother was horrified when she found out that one of the teachers tried to correct my sister's perfect pronunciation of Japanese to the accented Korean-Japanese. But other than that, we were perfectly happy at school. We got to know my class mistress so well that we used to correspond with her even after we returned to Japan. She used to write to us, promising that she would come to Japan to visit us when Japan hosted the Olympics. The Olympics never took place in the 1940s. Japan attacked Pearl Harbor in 1941 and the world was thrust into chaos.

Although the Japanese government forbade the use of the Korean language officially, by the time I went to school, they allowed a Korean language class in Korean schools. My mother, who did her best to discourage anything Korean, told me not to study it. My mother did not marry my father with the great political philosophy of creating a friendly relationship between Japan and Korea. If anything, she did not like anything Korean until I grew up and started influencing her with my objective attitude about both countries. I followed my mother's advice and just sat in Korean class without making much effort but I did pick up some Korean. I got 63% in one of the tests. I thought it was a great success. I did not even study and got 63%! So I climbed up the tree in front of our house with the test paper in one hand. I wanted the world to know that I could get 63% in Korean without studying it. I was waving it vigorously when Masao came home.

"Masao, Masao, look what a high mark I got in Korean," I called out.

"Oh, yeah? Let me see," he asked interestedly. I climbed down from the tree and showed him the paper, glowing with pride. "What?" he looked disappointed, "only 63%? I thought you got 100%."

I never adjusted to school life. I hated to do things with a group of people. At least I was going to a private school where the girls came from the same kind of background. It became even harder for me to adjust later when I had to go to a public school. One of the reasons I did not adjust easily was I was a mixture of two bloods and I did not feel a total affinity to either Japanese or Korean. So I was rather pleased when I took ill and had to stay home. It was even more welcoming because the weather had now changed to winter. The winter in Korea is severe. Cold wind blasted through the city of Seoul. It was a torture for me to get up early in the morning, wash with cold water and go out into the piercing cold wind. The name of my illness was tuberculous adenitis of the hilum—the first stage of tuberculosis.

In those days, contracting tuberculosis meant a death sentence. During the initial stage, one does not feel sick and the fever is not very high. One only feels constantly tired and a low fever of some 37 degrees persists. Since one does not feel very sick, one keeps on working or doing their normal tasks and the illness gets worse. In my case, I could take as much rest as I required because my mother was taking care of me. I was pleased with my great fortune of huddling in a warm room instead of venturing out into the cold weather. My elder sister, who always had to persevere against hardships of this type, went bravely like a warrior to school everyday. I, on the other hand, spent all day on the "ondoru". The "ondoru" is a unique Korean heating system. The floor was made of stone and covered by oil paper. The fuel hole was outside and everything burnable was thrown into it. My mother, who was used to healthy drafty Japanese houses, could not stand it. While she was pregnant with my younger sister, well-meaning relatives wanted to be nice to her and kept the "ondoru" as warm as possible. My mother nearly died. But I am half Korean so I loved it.

Now, one thing one must do while huddled in this "ondoru" room is to eat "reimyon" (cold noodles). The question arises "who will leave the comfort of this room and venture out to the shop?" Invariably, my father went out to buy the noodles while my mother prepared juice from "kimuchi"(Korean pickles) and set out bowls and chopsticks.

These are some vivid memories.

My mother was homesick for Japan. She often went to the edge of the hill and looked down into the city. Because of the Japanese oppression, the city had no life. It had a permanent air of sadness which enhanced my mother's heavy heart. In the distance, we could hear the terrible growl of tigers that were kept in the zoo. The booming cries of various animals echoed in the dusk and scared me.

Koreans never came up the hill where the Japanese were living but once a Korean woman clad in a white national outfit came screaming in Korean. She had a little girl with her who was trying to hide behind her skirt. We did not understand the meaning of what she was saying but we somehow gathered that some Japanese children teased her and the woman's love for her child gave her enough courage to come up the hill to confront the Japanese. My mother, as usual, went over to the woman and soothed her and gave her some food to make peace. The mother and daughter went home satisfied. After that, the little girl came up the hill from time to time, to see us. My mother always gave her something to eat, mainly white rice. One day my mother gave her some rice cooked with green peas. The little girl looked at the rice and slowly picked out the peas and threw them away. She had never seen green peas before.

On the way to school, at the foot of the hill, was a Chinatown. My elder sister and I used to have our hair cut at the barbershop that was located near the Chinatown. We were not posh enough to go to a hairdresser. I wonder if one existed in that area even if we had wanted to go to one. Most women did their own hair since the prevalent hair style was to pull it back and tie it in a chignon. My mother was sensitive to overgrown bangs on her children's heads since it made us look like neglected orphans (especially on my elder sister.) So she instructed my sister to stop at the barber shop on the way home from school to have it cut. But for some reason or another, she did not obey the instruction. For two days she came home with her overgrown bangs. My mother lost patience and gave her a strict order that it had to be cut.

The next day, my sister did not come home for a long time. The sky began to darken and it was clear that it would soon be completely dark. My mother already had been rushing in and out of the house to check if she could see her coming home or not. (It must have been when the weather was good. Otherwise she could not have rushed in and out of the house so easily.) I accompanied my mother, equally worried that my sister might have been kidnapped and sold to a Chinese circus. Being kidnapped and sold to a Chinese circus was one of the greatest worries of children at the time. We were well acquainted with the incredible acrobatic skills of the Chinese and the rigorous, almost cruel training that accomplished them. After running out of the house more than four times and with my mother's breath becoming short, we saw her. At the bottom of the hill, we saw her figure. As she came closer we noticed that her bangs were neatly trimmed. "Where have you been?" my mother shouted out of relief. Apparently, the barber's shop was crowded and she had to wait for a long time for her turn. "In that case, you should have waited till tomorrow." My mother lectured her about the use of common sense.

It was while I lived in Seoul that I saw lepers for the first time. There was a shrine at the bottom of the hill. Lepers, who were shunned by society, gathered there to beg. The Japanese, who built sanatoriums for their own lepers, did not bother for Korean lepers. They were simply abandoned and left to their own devices. One day, my mother, my elder sister and I happened to be in the vicinity of the shrine. One of the lepers noticed us and came closer. I think he noticed my mother's kimono and wanted to annoy this Japanese family, which we were not. Most lepers became vindictive because of their cursed affliction and were angry with their fate and with the world that had abandoned them. The leper was at a very serious stage of the disease. I remember that his attire was amazingly white. This whiteness sticks in my mind even today. He had already lost his hands and his face was completely disfigured and swollen with yellow pus.

The sight of him frightened us so much that I gasped and my mother's voice went up one octave higher, trembling. "Please go away, please go away," she pleaded while she quickly took out her purse to give him alms. I felt faint. When we finally got away, we were all pale and completely breathless. Together with fear, I felt deep sadness for a fate I could not help change.

The sight of this leper haunted me for years. I became keenly aware of this terrible disease. After we went back to Japan and when I was about ten or eleven, a Japanese female nurse wrote a book entitled "The Spring of the Island" (Kojima no Haru). She used to travel around the island, warning the people that leprosy was contagious and not hereditary as the majority of Japanese believed. Since a lot of Japanese believed that it was a hereditary disease, they dared to live together with lepers, sharing the crockery, beddings and baths and they believed that they were immune to the disease. She was also trying to get the patients to go into sanatoriums. Since the first stage of the disease is not very conspicuous and a leper does not like to be isolated, he or she would stay in society spreading the disease. The sad fact was that there was no cure for the disease until after World War II.

There are hundreds of tragic stories relating to leprosy. When I was about eleven, shortly before the outbreak of the Pacific War, I got hold of a book entitled "Who Walks Alone." It was written by an American physician in Nevada, who treated a man by the name of Ned Furgerson. This innocent ordinary American boy was drafted during the American-Spanish War of 1898. He was sent to the Philippines. After the victory of America over Spain, he had to stay on to fight the guerillas led by Aguinaldo. During his stay, he lived with a Filipino family for a year. He loved the family that consisted of the parents, a young pretty girl, named Alisa, and a young boy, called Sancho. He developed a special love for the family, especially for Alisa. After a year, he was called back home. Alisa promised to write but no letter came for almost a year. One day, the long-awaited letter arrived. She explained in the letter the reason why she had hesitated to write to him. Her brother, Sancho, had been diagnosed with leprosy. A cold shiver went down his spine. After all, he spent one whole year with them, living in the same house, eating from the same crockery.

For nine years nothing happened. Doubt and fear crossed his mind from time to time but he pushed it down to the lowest layer of his subconscious as if to shut the lid of a box that is too full to close. In the meantime, he fell in love with a nice American girl, named Jane, and got engaged. One day, there was a fire in the barn. One of his arms was badly burnt but he did not feel the pain. The doctor, who treated him, became suspicious. A test showed that Ned Furgerson was a leper.

He went into hiding. He secretly contacted his younger brother who came to see him. He gave his brother various instructions, including the strictest instruction not to tell his fiancée. Everything was going to be arranged so he could secretly disappear by faking his own death. He wanted to go back to the Philippines and spend the rest of his life in a sanatorium there. His kind physician arranged everything and he was to leave from New Orleans.

He traveled alone, secretly riding in a cargo train, always wearing gloves so that he would not spread the germs. He avoided all human contact. He could not make friends. One night he went to a park and sat down on a bench. He was desperately lonely. As he gazed at the starry sky, a street walker came and sat down next to him. "I am free tonight, you know," she said. He could not answer. His soul was crying out for human contact and crying with despair. But he was too conscientious to take advantage. So he sat in silence. She got up and left, throwing the departing words of "What an odd ball" at him. When I read the passage: "I was not allowed even to touch a prostitute," I broke down and cried. The suffering of this American man, a complete stranger, pierced my heart. His sorrows were a piece of glass that got stuck in my flesh and could not be taken out. Tears streamed down my cheeks without stopping.

Ned Furgerson arrived at the Filipino sanatorium and started his life as a leper. One day he ran into a beautiful female patient. It was Alisa. She was married but had been abandoned by her husband when he discovered that she, too, had contracted the disease. She was no longer the young fresh girl who giggled happily but she had grown into a beautiful mature lady. Since her disease had gone into remission, she was not disfigured in any way. She could not leave the sanatorium. Because of the stigma attached to leprosy, she would not be accepted back by society. So she remained at the sanatorium, helping the other patients.

Slowly they fell in love with each other. One night they made love and he proposed. She did not come back to give him an answer for some days. When she finally came to see him, she told him that she could not marry him. She was a Roman Catholic and the Church's teaching would not allow her to prevent the birth of children. If she had followed its teaching and had children, she would have to go through a heart-wrenching separation from them. She could not bear it. (The lepers' children were taken away from the parents and brought to the sanatorium from time to time to see the parents across the barbed-wire fence. A lot of tears were shed at each parting.)

After twenty-five years in the Philippines, Ned Furgerson decided to come home. As the train he was riding passed by the mountains of Nevada, his heart simply broke and died there. He had lost his hands to the disease but otherwise he was intact.

Also, at the foot of the hill, a vendor sold roasted chestnuts. Every year, my father's family back at the village sent us a big box of chestnuts and apples from their own trees and, of course, they selected the best ones for us. But to my sister and me, the vendor's chestnuts looked alluring. My mother kept on telling us that the chestnuts we got were far superior to the quality of the vendor's.

One day, however, we disobeyed our mother. For me, this was almost the only occasion in my entire life when I disobeyed my mother. I colluded with my sister to buy the vendor's chestnuts. I can't remember from where we got this five sen because usually we were not given any cash by our parents. Middle-class children never had cash. We certainly did not steal it. We trotted down to the chestnuts' vendor. The Korean man who was clad in a traditional costume gave us chestnuts in a tote made of newspaper. My sister and I ran away, giggling. We hurriedly cracked the shell of a chestnut and threw it into our mouths. But after one bite, our faces were twisted in disgust. We tried another one with the same result. We soon finished the whole tote. Every single chestnut was worm bitten and tasted bitter like our aching conscience. We spat all of them out. We learned a lesson that our mother was wise.

One night my sister and I lost our cherished beaded handbags our relatives gave us when we left the village. They were hanging from a nail stuck in a pillar of the house. During summer nights, I could see them from my bed, shimmering in the hazy moonlight. One night I opened my eyes but the night was empty. Our pretty beaded handbags were gone. Almost everyone in Korea was poor due to the Japanese oppression and there was a lot of theft. The thief must have thought that they were adults' handbags that contained money. I was disappointed but could not think badly of the thief.

One day, close to the end of the year, my mother clothed me warmly and sent me to school. All my classmates gathered around and fussed over me. One of them asked me in a kind tone: "Are you better?" I nearly cried because I knew I was not better. I was sent to school to say good-bye. We were going back to Japan. My father suggested that he could find a steady job in Seoul and have me looked after at the American hospital. My mother adamantly opposed his suggestion. We should go back to Japan and have me looked after by Japanese doctors. But in order to get out of Korea, my father had to pay debts. We had no money so we had to flit away during the night. To make the journey, my mother prepared three days of formula for my younger sister. My father packed all our belongings in three suitcases. Since I was sick, I could not carry anything. My elder sister may have been able to carry some things but she was also a child of eight years old. My mother's arms were occupied with the baby. So my father had to carry all three suitcases by himself.

I still remember that midnight at the Seoul railway station. The black train pulled in silently, looking formidable. The platform was deserted except for us. Unfortunately we were standing in the wrong spot. In order to get to the right door, we had to run. I saw my father run with three suitcases. He was young, tall, strong and reliable. We followed him. The train would stop for only a few minutes. We could not afford to miss the train lest the creditors would catch up to us. We somehow managed to scramble into a compartment. The train started moving immediately and soon picked up speed. Seoul retreated in darkness and the train ran ahead indifferent to the sentiments of the passengers.

Whenever I visualize my father with three suitcases, I feel a twist in my heart. He passed away at the age of 83. He was no longer capable of carrying three suitcases. One of the suitcases still sits in my storage room. It has been around the world, to Germany, to the U.S.A. and to Canada. "Has it got any memories?" I wonder.

I have passed through Seoul three times since then: in 1942, 1945 and not again until 1986.

chapter III

We were in Japan again. On the way back to Tokyo, we stopped in Osaka. In those days, trips by train were long and tedious. We needed a break and had to restock the baby's formula. The ferry ride and other parts of the journey are obscure in my memory. The next vivid memory is craning my neck waiting for dinner. In Osaka, we stayed at one of my father's acquaintances—free loading. To feed four mouths free was not a welcome phenomenon for the host's family, so our dinner did not come until late, until after the host's family had been fed. Perhaps the host wanted to show his displeasure by delaying our dinner as much as possible. As a child, I did not know that we were lucky even to be fed. I used to look out from the room allotted to us and jumped with joy when I saw the trays heading in our direction.

We arrived back in Tokyo towards the end of the year but again we had no place to go and no money. The only place offered to us was at my mother's male cousin's house. Most of my mother's relatives were doing well financially but Yokichi was the exception in the sense that he was poor and he was the only one who did not shun my mother after she had been disowned. Yokichi was the only son of my natural grandmother's sister. According to the Buddhist teaching, one's family's karma continues until it is resolved. It must be true. My grandmother was one of three sisters. My mother was one of three sisters and I am the middle one of three sisters. I don't mean to be boastful but good looks ran in this family. But by the time I got to know my great-aunt, she had lost her looks and had turned into a wizened old woman with a bent back and a mean character. She actually adopted my mother's eldest sister after my grandmother died. On her deathbed, when my grandmother learned that my aunt was going to be adopted by Yokichi's mother, she apparently said: "My sister hasn't got a nice character. I can't leave my child with her. Very soon, I will come back to fetch my child." She kept her promise. My aunt died at the age of sixteen. She was a pretty girl with thick glossy black hair. It was so rich and long, people had to push it into the coffin to close it. My mother used to say that she, with the worst hair—short, wavy and brownish—survived and the other two with beautiful hair died young. My great-aunt was thin and bony but had plenty of energy when it came to talking. She had a mean spirit and a smooth tongue. Her husband had died some time before. A tough life often gives a woman an undesirable character. Since Yokichi was the only child and son, she spoiled him rotten and dominated him at the same time. He was one of those people, who was good looking when he was young, but suddenly changed because his good looks were not supported by inner beauty. He was devastatingly handsome when he was young but by the time I got to know him, he had lost his good looks and was an ordinary common-looking fellow with very little education or culture. Our family and he had something in common. We were poor. My mother suspected that he was secretly coveting her adoptive father's wealth and tried to prevent reconciliation between her and her father. He probably thought that the inheritance might be passed onto him since he was the closest of kin. He was a jack-of-all-trades and master of none. He had dabbled in all kinds of occupations and succeeded in none. At the time, I think he was selling kimono material. He would load the rack on the back of his bicycle with his wares and visit his clients. He let me ride the bicycle sometimes, setting me on the bar in front of him and I thoroughly enjoyed the experience.

When our family, together with the baby, descended upon them, they were living in a rented house in working-class area or to be frank and politically incorrect, a low class area. I think there were only two or three rooms and we were squished into one of them and as a result they were equally squeezed into the rest of the space. By "they", I mean Yokichi, his mother, and his two daughters. Why there was no Mrs. Yokichi, I wondered even though I was a little girl. Soon I discovered why. Since Yokichi could not earn enough money, the heartless mother-in-law sent the poor woman to work in a Japanese inn. Once I saw the woman come home. She hesitated at the threshold as if it had been her master's house and she was a mere servant girl who was asking for permission to come in. Yokichi, the mama's boy, obviously did not feel much compassion for the woman's sacrifice as long as he could fix his mother's hair and generally run the household — including the cooking.

I hated the brown tatami mats in this house and the general atmosphere of poverty. If one had enough money, the surface of tatami mats would be renewed every year. A new tatami mat was green and had a pleasant fresh smell of the tatami grass. An old tatami, on the contrary, was brown and looked shabby. Obviously, the landlord did not bother to change the tatami mats for a long time since the house was situated in a lower class area and the family who rented it would not appreciate or take care of it. The life style downtown was entirely different from what I was used to. Since all the families in that area were poor, even the mothers did not have the luxury of staying at home, waiting for the husband's return from work in the evening and just looking after the family. Both husband and wife were working. As Toyohiko Kagawa, a famous evangelist put it: "True democracy exists in poor class." Since both husband and wife were earning money, they were on equal terms. Even the children were sent out to work at an early age. Sometimes the whole family was working at the same factory, with each member of the family earning the same amount of money.

The children, who were not working after school, were running around without parental supervision. If a family owned a small shop, the mother would be busy with the clients. So when the children came home from school, she couldn't be bothered with them. The easiest, and the simplest, solution was to give them five sen and tell them to go and play elsewhere.

To entertain such children, "kamishibai" (literally means paper theatre) came around every few days. A man mounts a small stage, similar to that of a puppet show. Instead of puppets, he had scenes of a story painted on cardboard sheets and told the story. He slid out each scene from the slit on the side of the stage. It was the old version of present-day slides, operated manually. The stories were always gaudy. A mean stepmother abusing and mistreating the stepdaughter was a favorite topic. Other stories were about a possessed cat that haunted a pretty young girl who would eventually be saved by a hero or some warriors conquering the apparitions of the evil spirits.

Each area in Tokyo has a patron shrine and an open space around it. This space was the usual gathering place. As the "kamishibai" man arrived on a bicycle with a stage tied to the back rack of the bike, he would go around clapping two wooden blocks together to let the children know that he was there. Children ran to the place, clutching five sen in hand. In return for five sen, one got a candy and the right to watch the paper theatre. Neither my sister nor I had five sen. Reason number one was we had no five sen to waste. Number two was my mother did not approve of our eating candies of inferior quality that coloured our saliva and turned our mouths red or yellow. Also, watching "kamishibai" was not in our life style. In our family, children should not run up to such vulgar entertainment.

The stories never ended at one showing. The man had to keep the children in suspense. So they would always end at some exciting moment. Thus, the children would need another five sen a few days later. Though my mother did not approve of it, I was fascinated by the stories. Once, I stayed on to watch a few scenes before the fellow shooed me away. He knew very well who had paid and who had not. I still remember the crude painting of a stepmother about to beat her stepdaughter, accompanied by the commentary given by the man in a suitable makeshift voice.

Yokichi's daughters were a little older than we and tried to convert us to their way of living. "Go and get the money from your Mom," they would command us. I could feel myself starting to run in the same manner as they did, to speak as they did and generally sinking to their lower level. Before we got entirely dyed by a different colour, my parents rescued us and moved to the "yamate" area (middle-class suburb). Here, even poverty was in a different form. Instead of the whole family going to work, the wife stayed home because it was a shame for a man not to be able to support his family. They endured poverty in a higher style and with vain pride.

We rented a small house next to the landlady. In that household, there were only two women, a widowed mother and her daughter. In the days where women totally depended on men to support them, the lot of a widowed woman was not good. The pension often was a pittance and the women had no particular skill by which they could earn money. Fortunately, these women owned the house we were renting.

There was no aqueduct system in the house. We had to draw water from the well that was between the two houses. My mother hated to go out and bump into the neighbors. My mother, who was pure Japanese, never learned to deal with other Japanese. She also never acquired the technique to deal with neighbours. One thing she believed firmly was: "They all look down on me because I am a Korean's wife." True, there was a lot of racial prejudice but it should not be an excuse for everything. Even among the Japanese themselves, there was backbiting, bickering and meanness. Maybe because I am actually half Korean, I did not care so much about what the Japanese said. My attitude was: "So? It is not my fault. There is nothing wrong with being Korean. I will, one day, become such a fine person that your words won't affect me." Does meanness and jealousy stop if one is Japanese and has a high position? I don't think so. One can't change human nature. As long as the earth exists and human beings are on it, things will not change. Some exterior circumstances change, for instance, women get suffrage and blacks are integrated in schools, but true prejudice still exists and will do so till the end of the world. Why should I be unhappy because of other people's opinion, let alone when it's not correct?

Since my mother wanted to avoid contact with the neighbours, she sent me, one day, with a fifty sen coin to the landlady's house to have it broken into small change. It seemed to escape her mind that if she, an adult, did not like dealing with neighbours, a child of seven might not like it even more. But I did not mind running the errand. When I knocked on the door, the older lady came out and did what I asked. I gazed at five ten sen she placed in my hand and returned to her one coin. "I think this belongs to you," I said. She smiled: "No, you don't have to give it to me."

I pondered for a few seconds. Then it dawned on me that since I did not buy anything from her, I did not have to pay her anything. I nodded and bowed politely: "Thank you very much." She did not look like a horrible woman to me.

One of the reasons my mother could not stand others was that she could never stand her ground without getting into trouble. In those days, it was a rare house that locked the front door unless it was a mansion where there were a lot of things to steal or when one went out for a long time. So, any visitor could open the front door and say: "Gomenkudasai" (Excuse me, hello). If one heard no answer, one would simply leave. This meant anybody who wanted to drop in, could drop in and sit on the wooden stoop and chat as long as one wished. My mother was completely devoid of the technique of getting rid of unwanted guests. She was afraid that the upset visitor would attribute everything to her being a Korean's wife. As I grew older, I would come out to meet the visitor or stick my head out in the middle of unending chatter to warn my mother that the rice was boiling over and I did not know what to do with it. She must come inside and give me instruction. Strangely enough, although I was a mere child, the Japanese, even the adults, were afraid of me and the visitor would cut the chatter short and leave. The foreign blood I had in me must have had a strange effect. The visitor also must have sensed my contempt for useless chatter.

Soon after we settled in our rented house, the New Year came round. But we had no money. We didn't even have a table to set the plates on. So we got a wooden crate used for packing mandarin oranges from a green grocer and turned it upside down and used it as a table.

On New Year's Day, my parents swallowed their pride and sent my elder sister and me to my grandparents who had disowned my mother for marrying a Korean. It is customary in Japan to pay courtesy visits to relatives and friends; nice uncles and aunts would give money put in special envelopes to younger members of the family. I somehow sensed the true meaning of this mission. So, off we trotted to our grandparents. Their house lay some distance from where we lived. There was no direct public transportation, so we walked. Next thing I remember, we were standing in the foyer of their house, warmly clad in hand-knitted sweaters and woolen overcoats. At the sound of our entry, my grandmother came out. When she saw us, she made a little cry, "Ah—." My sister and I chanted out a duet of "shinnen omedeto gozaimasu" (Happy New Year). She knew why we came. She disappeared into the inner core of the house and we could hear whispering sounds. They must have been discussing how much to give. A few minutes later, she reappeared with a money envelope. I forgot how much they gave us but it must have been enough to keep us going for a while. My mother apparently went to beg a few more times but my grandmother told her not to come. My grandmother, she said, was reminded of the happy days every time she came and it broke her heart. She could not bear it. Poor grandmother! Now I understand how she must have felt. I cry for both of my grandmothers.

Actually, this was not the only time I saw my mother's parents. Shortly before we went to Korea, we were invited to visit them properly. I can't remember whether my father was invited or not. But my grandfather gave my sister and me Japanese dolls. I take to everyone, so I jumped around, talking to him without any reservation and was genuinely happy to receive a doll. But my elder sister, who was difficult with strangers, would not look at him, let alone speak to him and proved to be generally unloving. My grandfather threatened that he would not give her the doll. A rather unsophisticated approach from the viewpoint of child psychology and education but he was not so well educated and lacked the knowledge of "what not to do with children". "No, I don't want it." She was equally obnoxious. But in the end, she got the doll, too.

Years later, when I was a pre-teen, my grandfather took ill and he thought of reconciliation again. We went to see him at the hospital but he decided not to take us back into his family. He said my mother, by that time, belonged to a totally different class and there was no longer an emotional bond between them. My poor grandfather could not trust anyone to whom he could give his estate. True, there were some who actually coveted his money but not my father. My father would have been genuinely nice to him because he had a nice big heart. My grandfather eventually took in my cousin who was born to my mother's middle sister and had been orphaned quite young. I don't think either of them was happy. My father felt sorry for the young girl and tried to see her several times but my mother dissuaded him because his action might be misinterpreted as an interest in the inheritance. After World War II ended and when we naturalized ourselves as Japanese, my father came back from the registry office and said to my mother: "Your parents are both registered as dead." My heart aches to know what happened to them during the time we were not in contact with them.

While we were at this house, my elder sister burned herself. My mother was out and my sister was carrying my younger sister on her back and the hem of her dress caught the kettle that was boiling over the charcoal in the brazier. Hot water poured onto her thigh. When my mother came home and found out what had happened, her face turned white. She diligently washed her thigh with soy sauce, which was believed to be the best treatment for burns. In those days, most ailments were treated at home. Ordinary people did not go to a doctor unless something was drastically wrong. Very fortunately, the burn healed without a scar.

It was during this time that my younger sister, Keiko started walking. She was clad in a wool suit my mother knitted and took her first wobbly step in the garden. I think I was the first person to witness it. "Mummy!" I called out. "She walks!" There was a lot of joyful commotion. My mother sent me out to a shoe store nearby to buy a pair of shoes. None of us had enough sense to measure her feet so the first pair of shoes I brought back was too small. I rushed back to the store to exchange them. When I returned with another pair of shoes, they fit. We made a fuss of putting her little feet into the shoes and held her hands to help her walk.

It was also while we were at this house that the famous coup d'état took place. The night before February 26, 1936, Tokyo was buried under a thick blanket of snow. All transportation stopped functioning and the city was completely disabled. In the early morning of the 26th (around 5 a.m.), young military officers under the leadership of lieutenant Kurihara revolted against the government that had been trying to suppress the ever-growing power of the military. They went on a rampage of killing pacific politicians. They invaded the prime minister's residence, shot the guards and the policemen, and tried to assassinate the ruling prime minister, Keisuke Okada. Fluky luck saved him, for the rebels mistook his brother-in-law for him, killed him and thought they had succeeded in killing the prime minister. But Okada was hiding in the closet in the maid's room, while the maid sat in front of the closet, guarding him. The rescuers tried to get him out of the residence. The two secretaries, Sekomizu and Fukuda, got permission from the leader of the rebels to invite some mourners to pay their respects to the corpse of the prime minister, which was actually his brother-in-law's. When the mourners arrived, they were told to sit and wait in the next room. In the meantime, the maid managed to get his morning dress out of the wardrobe and put it on the prime minister so that he would look like one of the mourners. The morning dress was the standard formal outfit for men during the day for any kind of ceremony in Japan. Okada wore the morning dress, glasses and a huge white mask (a common custom in Japan during the winter to defend oneself against catching colds). When they passed by the two rebel soldiers at the entrance, Fukuda, one of the secretaries, ostentatiously scolded the prime minister for looking at the corpse ; that's why he felt faint. As soon as he got outside, Fukuda motioned the first car in the cue to come up and pushed Okada into it and told the chauffeur to drive on. Whoever owned the car would not have been able to use it when he came out. He would have wondered how it had disappeared.

The rebels hoped to establish a totally military government with the emperor's sanction. However, they had miscalculated the emperor. Contrary to the general belief in the West, Emperor Hirohito was a pacifist. He had been trying in vain to curb the power of the military. He had appointed several pacific civilian prime ministers, asking them to help him maintain peace. Unfortunately, the pacifists all became targets of assassination. The storming of the prime minister's residence and the attacking of Okada by the military was but one of the examples. In this coup d'état, the other two pacific politicians were not so fortunate and lost their lives. The emperor made his position clear by calling them rebels and not the patriots they aspired to be called.

On the 29th of February, the rebels were suppressed. Only one of the ringleaders committed "harakiri" and the rest were court-martialled. The Japanese promised to commit "harakiri" if Japan lost World War II, but at the end of the war, only one military officer (a true patriot who worked for the emperor) committed it.

The year after this incident, 1937, Japan invaded China. I remember my father saying that this would make the position of the Chinese in Japan very difficult. They had already been looked down upon and treated with prejudice. But Japan soon established a puppet government in the Japanese-occupied area in China, and a lot of Chinese stayed in Japan and carried on with their lives.

We soon moved to another house which was about a block away. The house was brighter and a little bigger. It was a duplex and the neighbor who rented the other half of the duplex was a widow by the name of Kojima. I do not know how she was earning a living but she must have been working herself to the bone in order to send her only son to a university. Since her life was so hard, she could not cultivate a nice character. After we moved in, ticks started attacking us. Since the Kojima living quarters were connected by the ceiling with ours, the ticks had free passage from one place to the other. We didn't know from which house they originated. The landlord's house was situated on the other side of our house. Mrs. Kojima promptly went to the landlord to complain that the Korean neighbors were generating ticks. The landlord and his wife were nice people without prejudice and apologized to us for her behavior. My father and Mr. Horii got along well because they were on the same wavelength intellectually. Unfortunately, the ticks had no racial prejudice and they attacked us as well as the Japanese. We were itching and scratching madly and tried several methods to expel the pests without any success. Finally, my mother resorted to the drastic method. She fumigated the whole house with formalin, a deadly liquid, while we went out for a walk. The ticks were destroyed but it nearly destroyed us, too. For some reason, she did not dispose of the liquid immediately and kept it in a closet. I, when I had to put my socks away, was afraid of the dark so I hurled them into the closet without looking. One of the socks fell into the container of formalin and fumes of lethal gas started rising from the closet. My mother noticed the smell and hurriedly disposed of it, shouting at us all to get out and breathe fresh air. I was so nervous that my legs trembled and I could not put on my shoes. I remember my foot kept on slipping out of a shoe despite my efforts. My mother had to look after my younger sister and had no time to look after the older ones. It was dark outside but the air was fresh. I held tightly to one sleeve of my mother's kimono, savoring the feeling that I had escaped death.

Mrs. Kojima, who was battling so hard to make something out of her son, died suddenly of an illness, soon after her son graduated from university and got a job. Poor woman! Apparently her last words were: "I don't want to die, I don't want to die." Surely, she must have wanted to live. I feel for her now that I am an adult. How she must have wished to enjoy the fruit of her sacrifices. I pray that she will have a better life in the next life.

While we were at this house, my father must have had a steady job. Our personal life was quite settled and the result of the Japanese invasion of China was not yet so obvious. My father, who was always eager to learn something new, started taking a correspondence course in brush writing. I still remember his spreading paper on a table (we had one then) and grinding the ink stone. When the ink was dark enough, he first practiced on newspaper. When he thought the writing was good enough, he wrote it on a piece of good paper. Then he sent it to the teacher. It came back with corrections in red ink. I remember my father sitting at the table with his limbs sticking out of his cotton kimono. The material of a kimono was sold in a fixed length and it was never enough for my father who was Korean and much taller than an average Japanese man.

This house did not have an aqueduct system either. Very fortunately, the well was inside the house but the quality of the water was bad. It had to be purified. First we had to get a big wooden barrel and place pebbles and palm leaves inside it. As we poured the brown water from the well into it, the water slowly permeated through the pebbles and palm leaves and came out from the spout, looking clean. The previous well was a trolley and bucket type but this one was a little more modern, pumping type. Pumping the water all day for housekeeping and filling up the bathtub was not an easy job. My mother started suffering from rheumatism. So we had to share the task of pumping. One of the reasons why pumping water was so difficult for my mother was that she was small and the pumping gear was above her; whereas my elder sister and I are half Korean and tall and the pumping handle was lower for us.

There was also a little yard at the back of the house and there was a raspberry bush. When summer came the raspberry trees bore plenty of red sweet berries. Since I had a Korean stomach and was always hungry, I crouched in the bush and ate most of the berries by myself. I was fortunate to have an elder sister who was picky about food. She did not invade my territory. My mother even ventured out to plant some strawberries in the yard. She told me that it would take one whole year until they would bear fruit. I remember saying to myself: "A whole year!" One year was an eternity for a young child. But a year soon passed and I was able to eat the red ripe strawberries.

chapter IV

*A*s we came back from Korea, my elder sister and I transferred to a Japanese public school. Children were assigned to a particular school according to the area where they lived. To walk to the nearest school, it took us about forty minutes. We had a backpack made of leather. We packed textbooks, notebooks and a pencil case. At one corner of the backpack, a ruler stuck out. When we had a calligraphy class, we had to carry an extra paper case so that the paper would not get crumpled. On a rainy day, this extra packet was a nuisance. On a rainy day (it rains often in Japan), we had to put on a rubber raincoat with a hood, rubber boots and carry an umbrella. In this outfit, with an umbrella and a packet in our hands, to walk for forty minutes to school was a chore. At the age of seven or eight, it was a great struggle. My elder sister who was imbued with the mission of being the eldest, called out to me: "Walk behind me, walk behind me." Thus she tried to be a human shield to protect me from the cruel natural elements.

Every year, Japan regularly gets hit by typhoons that come up from somewhere in the Southeast Asian Sea. Once school was dismissed because the heavy rain did not stop all morning and the school was afraid that the streams that ran in the area would overflow and the children would not be able to cross over to get back home. I was walking towards home as quickly as possible. As I came by one of the streams, the height of the brown water surprised me. It was nearly touching the bridge that spanned over it. The water that was usually calm and clear, was whirling around in a brown rage. This sudden fury of nature scared but also fascinated me. I stood there for a few seconds and watched it, dazed.

Again another time, the rain was accompanied by fierce wind. On the way to school, there was a slight hill and on the top of the hill, stood a solitary pine tree. As I was coming home, a gust of wind tried to blow my umbrella away from my hands. I wisely shut it and carried it home. But my elder sister who lacked such wisdom, threw away the umbrella (she was not with me at the time; we came home at different times) at the foot of the pine tree and came home empty handed. I still remember my mother's grimace. Such umbrellas could be easily repaired for little money. It would cost a lot more money to buy a new one and my family was not that well off. My mother who never scolded us for losing coins when we were sent on errands or any other losses caused by mistakes, did not scold her but half laughed and half cried. My father who was also casual about the loss of material goods, laughed. I think he went to the spot where my sister had abandoned her umbrella to retrieve it but someone had already picked it up.

When I first entered the school, it was during the last semester of the first year. Very fortunately, I had a nice female teacher by the name of Machida. The Japanese school year started in April and ran until about the 23rd of July. August was summer holidays and the second semester ran from September to about the 23rd of December. The New Year's holidays ended on the seventh of January. The third semester covered January to about the 23rd of March.

The first day of the school, we had a singing class. In those days, at elementary schools, every classroom had a little harmonium and every teacher was required to accompany the children's singing. It was a part of the curriculum at the Teachers' Training College to learn to play harmonium. I can't remember whether all male teachers could manage this skill but all the female teachers did and a few of the male teachers certainly could. Mrs. Machida asked a few children to sing solos. After I had sung, she praised me and asked me to sing again to demonstrate to the class how the song should be sung.

But I did not do so well in calligraphy class. The Korean school's standard of curriculum was a bit behind that of the Japanese schools. This was my first time handling an ink stone, an ink stick and paper. After I spread out the gear on the desk, I watched the girl next to me and tried to imitate her. I ground the ink and dipped the brush in the ink stone and scrawled the letters, glancing at the sample book placed at my left. After several attempts, one must submit the writing one thought best to the teacher so she could mark it. In order to do this, one must write one's full name at the left hand corner. So I made my best effort and carefully wrote out my Korean name, "Boku Aiko."

The girl next to me saw it. She immediately changed her attitude and sneered: "You, Korean? What a funny name! Ha! Ha! Ha!" I, being half Korean, did not crumble down in tears as Japanese girls would have done. In silence, I dipped my brush into the ink stone, raised it and drew circles on her face. Since the brush was saturated with ink, her cheeks turned black. She never expected this kind of counter attack. She burst out crying. Tears are water. Water mingled with the black ink on her face and started dripping down in drops. She wiped her face with calligraphy paper but did not quite succeed. I can't remember what happened after that. I still don't know why the teacher did not reprimand me. Maybe it was the end of the school day and we packed up. I still remember the girl's crying face and my Korean name on the paper in terrible writing. I went home worried that the school might send a notice to my parents. As I was walking towards home, one of the classmates came up to me to console me. Maybe she, too, was suffering from this mean girl. I tried to explain to her about the injustice but I somehow was not convinced. Maybe because I was aware of the terrible Korean temperament I possessed and found difficult to control.

Since this was a public school, it consisted of mainly the children from the lower middle class. A lot of the fathers were engaged in menial work or owners of small shops. The parents were working hard, earning little. This was the day when the class distinction was apparent. The Royal Family was revered. There was still a legal distinction between the nobility and the commoners. The military had a hard grip on the government and the public. The children from the lower classes were tough as weeds. They not only had physical strength but also a toughness of spirit. The parents were too busy to worry about their children so they sent them to school even if they had a cold and a little fever. There was no space in their lives for any kind of idling. While my classmates came to school, sneezed, coughed, and got rid of it, I caught the cold at the sound of their sneezing and had to stay in bed for at least a week. I learned a lesson from this. If one wants to remain healthy, don't study the symptoms and worry about the diseases. Indifference to them keeps one healthy. Then I got healthier. But in those days, my mother's over-sensitivity was contagious. I worried about faint coughing and a little sneezing and I got sick immediately.

In those days, poverty meant poverty. No money meant no money. There was no such thing as government support or subsidies. Since most children in public schools were poor, they wore the same clothes to school everyday. During school semesters there were several national holidays: "Kigensetsu" (Birthday of the country) on February 11, "Tenchosetsu" (Emperor's Birthday—at the time the emperor was Showa) on April 29th, "Meijisetsu" (birthday of Emperor Meiji, the deceased grandfather of Emperor Showa) on November 3rd and New Year's Day. On such occasions the children went to school only in the morning for the assembly and the rest of the day was a holiday.

A small theatre frame, that resembled a puppet show stage with a curtain drawn in front of it, was erected behind the school principal who stood on the platform. Behind the curtain was a photograph of the emperor and empress. The principal, with white-gloved hands, would reverently unroll the scroll and read the Emperor Meiji's edict on education to us. It began with "chin omouni" (the emperor's way of saying: "I think..."). When the recitation was finished, he would roll up the edict and put it away. Then he would pull the string of the curtain in a most revered manner. The curtain would slide to both sides, parting in the middle. But as soon as he started pulling the string, we were to bow so deeply and with great awe so that our eyes would not commit the crime of disrespect by looking at it for the emperor was a descendant of gods and he was a god.

Blood is a funny thing. Just because I was half Korean, without being taught, I knew it was all a bunch of fiddlesticks. I never believed that the emperor was a god. Why did Emperor Meiji and Emperor Taisho die if they were gods? Anybody who dies is not a god—that was my belief. I kept it to myself. I kept a lot of things to myself because it was dangerous to voice dissident ideas. When I was in fourth grade, I lost patience and was determined to have a look at the photograph. I scoffed at the idea of one's going blind if one looked at the descendant of gods. Very fortunately, I was tall and was standing at the very back row. As soon as the principal started pulling the string and everybody else's head bent downwards, I raised mine half way up and had a good look at the photograph. It was an enlarged version of the one in our history textbook.

I abhor people who try to oppress the public with their narrow-minded righteousness and I despise people who have no opinion of their own. Millions of Japanese followed the military like obedient sheep. Even as a child I did not.

There is a very tragic story concerning the royal photograph. The father of a famous novelist was a principal of a school that unfortunately had a fire. The emperor's photograph perished in this fire. The principal was held responsible for not rescuing the photograph and he committed suicide.

On such holidays, however, each child was given a packet of two cakes that tasted awful. One cake was dark pink and the other white. The children, who could afford it, wore a new dress. Those, who could afford new dresses, were the upper crust of the class. My mother, who was skilled in sewing and imbued with the idea that she had to prove to the world that Koreans were not always dirty and low class, made new dresses for my sister and me, every time a feast day came around. She worked furiously. Since we did not have enough money to plan new dresses ahead of time, she had to make two dresses in two or three days right before the feast day. They were all hand sewn. My father chose the material. My mother used to say that the material he chose did not look nice as material but when it was sewn up as dresses it looked much better than the material she would have chosen. I think it was because my father was more used to the western concept of dresses. One year, just before the New Year came around, my father could not get money for our new dresses until about two days before the New Year. My mother cut and sewed two dresses, sitting up all through the night. I was bored, trying on the dress over and over again until it fitted. But I was proud to go to school and have the teachers and my friends ask me: "How lovely! Did your mother make that, too?" Some of my classmates said to me: "I envy you." I felt a tinge of sadness about the social injustice. I was never haughty about my looking better or possessing something that was better than what they had.

There was another girl in my class who belonged to this upper class. Her name was Hiroko. She was the daughter of an army captain. On feast days, she came to school in a black velvet dress with a white lace collar. Her parents genuinely had no prejudice against me. Her mother, on the contrary, wanted Hiroko to associate with me rather than with other Japanese girls. At one point, she pressured the teacher to let her and me sit next to each other. This ended in a fiasco. We, mainly I, yapped all through the classes and finally the teacher had to separate us again. At the end of the semester, I presented my parents with a report card with "otsu (B)" in conduct. It was customary for Japanese schools to give "ko (A)" to everyone unless a pupil went drastically out of line. So this "otsu" meant more than a simple "B".

Hiroko's family also was the only other family, besides mine, that invited the child's friends to their home. Once, four or five classmates, including me, were invited for her birthday party. Their house was in a decent area and I could tell that the family had a certain standard. While I was there, I saw a photograph of Hiroko's father in an army officer's uniform and as I looked out to the garden, an elderly gentleman, obviously Hiroko's grandfather, was crossing the garden with a pot of plants in his hands. I felt, even as a child, that he must have had a rather stern character. Later I found out that he was a retired navy officer. Hiroko's mother lived with the in-laws. I did not envy her life and this was the kind of married life I was going to avoid.

In those days, if one asked a boy, "What would you like to be when you grow up?" a lot of them would have answered: "An army general" or "A navy admiral" or something similar. But I had absolutely no desire to do anything with the military. I was half Korean. I had no country for which I wanted to die and I would never have died for Japan. On the whole I would never die for an ideology.

Hiroko, a daughter of an army captain and a granddaughter of a navy officer, was the most uncoordinated child in the whole class. Obviously, the family expected her to excel in physical activities as well as in intellectual subjects. She was intelligent and a hard worker. She held about fourth place out of sixty children whereas I was about the ninth. I did not like physical education so I avoided it as often as I could. I had an aversion to exposing my thighs in a pair of blue bloomers and hanging from an iron bar. I had a good excuse. I was still suffering from the aftermath of the illness.

I was terrible at running. I was the tallest girl in the whole school with the longest legs, yet those short Japanese girls always beat me. I was always at the end of the line. I only joined the class when I could wear a nice pleated skirt for dancing. But Hiroko tried. I think the family instilled into her the spirit of perseverance, a Japanese virtue. Her legs and arms seemed to move differently and her legs moved in a peculiar swirling motion. Some children jeered at her but she would not give up. She did not even cry. She tried.

After six years of elementary school, some of us, who could afford further education, had to take an entrance examination for a secondary school. The ministry of education had just changed the system. We were to be judged solely by our transcripts. I was going to go to a Protestant Christian school that my elder sister had entered the year before. I would not even have dreamed of going to a school that was imbued with militaristic ideas. Hiroko, however, being a daughter of an army captain, had to go to a government-run school. Such schools, however, lay importance on excellence in physical activities as well as on the intellectual. She was not accepted. I think it was due to the poor marks in physical education. She had to go to a private school with a lower standard whose examination date was placed after that of government schools. The schools, that were not so prestigious in the public eye, would set the examination date later than the famous ones so that they could act as a saving factor for those who failed in their first choice. In the end I went to a better school than she did because my first choice was the school that was not very famous but very good and later the school became very famous as well.

I sometimes wonder what happened to her. At the end of World War II, her father would have lost his job, if he had not been killed. Her grandfather's pension would have ceased. Her whole family must have had a hard time as a result of the war. I wish her well.

When I was in Grade Two, something that changed my whole life happened. I discovered the world of books. One day it rained. In Japanese schools, on rainy days, the children had no place to go and play. We were allowed to stay in the classrooms. On this particular day, however, instead of letting the children run wild and do whatever we liked, the class mistress made us sit in our seats and she read a story to us. It was a story from "Grimm Fairy Tales," I discovered later. It opened my eyes to a world that was full of spiritual riches.

Very unfortunately, the recess was over soon and the story ended in the middle. Desire to know what happened at the end of the story nearly drove me crazy. I must have found out from the teacher the name of the book because soon my mother bought me seven volumes of "Grimm Fairy Tales." From then on I was hooked on books. Reading became the main object and food of my life. In Japan, in those days, in order to read books decently, one had to learn thousands of Chinese characters. I learned them from the books I was reading. As a result, I excelled in Japanese classes. I also started writing. When I was in Grade 3 and 4, my composition was chosen to be printed in the school magazines. This had a special meaning because a Korean surname had never appeared in such magazines before.

I was so immersed in books that the wise teacher put me in charge of the school library. I sat in the room, devouring one book after another, while waiting for someone to come and take out books. No one came. So I read in peace. When the time came to pack up, the school was deserted and the sky was turning into late afternoon. Sometimes I read while I was walking.

Once, my mother sent me out to a grocery store to buy pepper. On the way to the store, I ran into my sister's classmate. Knowing that I loved reading, she said to me: "This month's issue of Shojo (Young Girls) Club just arrived. You may read it first." I gladly followed her to her house and got the magazine. A second later, my nose was deeply buried in it.

I forgot about the errand. I went home with the magazine instead of the pepper. My mother was very annoyed. But she did not send me out again.

Apart from the fact that she had to stay home with my younger sister, she sent us on errands liberally because her legs were shorter than ours and she could not walk as fast as we could. In those days, the only transit system in the suburb was our legs. Buses ran infrequently and were very inefficient. However, once one got to the railroad station, the transit system was very good.

I soon ran out of reading material in the children's section and started exploring my mother's women's magazines. My mother could not quite make up her mind whether she should let me continue reading them or stop me because in those days, one did not even discuss any kind of relationship between a man and a woman in front of children. They were supposed to be kept innocent until about the time of marriage. At first she tried to go along with the traditional teaching. So she hid the magazines. I knew where they were—between the folds of the comforters in the closet. When my mother was busy in the kitchen or washing in the bathroom, I pulled them out from the hiding place and read them. As I was a tremendously fast reader, I could finish reading them by the time she finished doing whatever she was doing. One day she caught me reading them. After a feeble attempt to hide them again, she gave up. I think she was too busy and couldn't be bothered.

Once she ordered a set of four hard cover books called "Ogasawara School of Manners." The books were fascinating reading material. The "Ogasawara School" was the ultimate authority on manners. It taught us the strict code of manners and etiquette: what to wear on what occasion, what to do on making visits and how to act at a wedding. It taught us how to behave in front of dignitaries and how to conduct ourselves when we received certificates at the end of a semester or on other occasions: namely, how to proceed by sliding our feet, how to bow, how many times and how to step aside. In the section on weddings, there was an instruction in obtuse language about how women should conduct themselves on their wedding night. It stirred my curiosity. I was beginning to sense something about the relationship between a man and a woman. At the same time, by reading everything I could lay my hands on, I knew a lot more about how to protect myself against sexual assault than other children. There was also a section on how to behave at a dance party. It warned the lady not to start leading the gentleman even if he was a clumsy dancer.

In those days, six years of elementary school education were compulsory. Since there were no such luxuries as special schools or counsellors, children with mental disabilities, epilepsy or any other problems were enrolled in public schools. They attended schools for six years and received a graduation diploma at the end, whether they had learned anything or not. As long as they were present physically and could write their names on examination papers, they were promoted from one grade to the next. There were about three girls in my class, who obviously had some mental problem. One girl especially stood out as someone who needed help. But the parents had neither the knowledge nor the money to take this girl to a specialist for help. Everyday, she came to school faithfully and stood at the corner of the playground staring vacantly. She wore the same dress over and over again. One day, however, she turned up in a new skirt. A skirt was cut and sewn in the fashionable style, with straps crossed behind her. The material was some thick wool in a sombre colour. I could tell that the mother had made the utmost effort and summoned all her skill to make this skirt. Only she was not as skilled as my mother and did not know how to finish the hem. I still remember the thread hanging down from the hem of the skirt. Even as a child, though, I could feel the tragic heroic desire of the mother to make a new skirt for the child she loved and I was deeply impressed.

In a lower grade, there was also a boy, who had epilepsy. He had a foul temper and once aroused, he would throw terrible tantrums. So the teachers did not restrain him even though he went out of the classroom at his will, roamed around the school or weaved in and out of the columns of children during the morning assembly. But when he was calm, he was quite intelligent. We all tried not to tread on his toes in order to avoid his tantrums. Just once I witnessed his seizure. He lay on the ground with foams of saliva spilling out of his mouth. I was scared out of my wits.

When I was a child people did not clean up life. They did not immediately put away the mentally disabled or the ones with epilepsy. We somehow lived together with the problems, making the best out of them. By doing so we learned about the dark corners of life and the skill of coping with difficult phases of life. Life was not all sunny. We did not expect someone else to come and rescue us. The family stuck together and found happiness in little triumphs and that was life.

chapter V

*I*n those days, even in Tokyo, the suburbs still had not been developed and there were quite a few vacant lots where children could gather and play. Sometimes, a stray dog would come and join us. In front of our rented house, there was a sizable lot and my elder sister and I used to take our younger sister, Keiko, there in a pram. On one evening, while she was in the pram, Keiko had a temper tantrum. She wanted something and we did not give it to her. She stood up in the pram with a face as red as a boiled lobster and fists tightly clenched. Since she stood up in one end of the pram, it became unbalanced and tipped over, throwing her down on the ground. Even as children, we knew that hitting one's head hard against a solid object was not good for the brain. Sakae and I turned pale with worry and were later relieved to find that there was no damage done to her brain. (We think.)

In the corner house, two houses down from us, there lived a family of four women: the mother and three daughters. The two elder sisters were unmarried because of their younger sister. She was mentally retarded. When a family has a member with defects like that, nobody in that family is able to get married. No marriage go-between would bring marriage proposals. People in the Orient lay importance on blood. Also, the family would look after the handicapped and would sacrifice their own lives as long as that person lived.

They were a family of means. They owned a house and had a reasonable standard of living. The middle daughter, Masako, was an English teacher and was earning money in a decent, lady-like manner. In the days when women did not get a higher education, she was a graduate of Tsuda College, a noted ladies' educational institute for the study of the English language.

Hearing Keiko's scream, Miss Sasaki rushed out of the house. She examined Keiko's head and generally consoled us all. I noticed her skin was smooth, fair and beautiful. Despite the fact that she was one of the "old maids", she was cheerful and kind and looked happy and content. Later, I learned the reason for her nice disposition. She was a Christian and later, when I attended Keisen Girls' School, she became my English teacher.

One day, labourers appeared to prepare the ground of the vacant lot. This was a sign that a house was going to be built. At first, they built something similar to a May Queen pole. A big log was erected in the center and from its top hung several ropes in about ten directions. Each labourer would hold the end of a rope and altogether pull up the log with a loud cry of "enya kora" and release it. The log would hit the ground with a thud. They would repeat the same movement in one spot until the earth became firm and they would move to another spot. Thus, they went around the lot until the earth was firm enough for building a house.

Sometimes women were working as "yoitomake" (labourers who did this kind of job were called by this name). The woman, who came to work on the lot in front of our house, was of small build, gentle and feminine and not at all toughened by rough life. Her white teeth showed in her brown face as she smiled and joked with her male co-workers.

Since the houses in the suburbs were far from the shops, errand boys from various shops: the meat shop, fish shop, green grocery and the sake shop that sells soy sauce, came around every morning to take orders. They were young fellows, usually in their late teens. They came with a thick notebook, stood at the back door next to the kitchen and wrote down the order. The goods were delivered in the afternoon before the housewife started cooking dinner. Sometimes romance blossomed between one of the young fellows and a maid employed by the household.

Tofu vendors came around, carrying tofu in wooden tubs that hung from the hooks at the ends of a pole which they carried on their shoulders. As they went around the streets, they would call out: "Tofu, Tofu" or something similar. When a housewife heard the call, she would call out: "Tofuya sa—n" to let the vendor know that he was needed and she would rush out with a container and money to buy tofu and other soy bean products.

A welder came around, too. He would repair kettles, cooking pots and anything else that leaked or had broken into pieces. He would light up the acetylene gas that was placed in one corner of his stall. A flame burst out, accompanied by blue smoke and I was fascinated. After his work was finished, all the kettles stopped leaking and the cooking pots were usable again.

Other vendors came along from time to time and filled the various needs of the households. The medicine man from Toyama selling bears' gut for the cure of gastric ailments was a well-known figure. There was a lot of rushing out to do for a housewife. My mother relied on my quick legs and I performed the duty of calling the vendors for her. In those days, young children of nine or ten were more useful than children of today, not just in Japan but everywhere.

Tatami workers came to change the surface of tatami mats. The artisan would set up a wooden frame, upon which he laid a mat of tatami in order to rip off the edge and the old surface of the mat. Then, he would place a new clean tatami surface and edge and sew them onto the backing.

He had a protective black patch on one elbow as he used his elbow to press down the edge and adjust the tension of the thread. A large silver needle went in and out of the tatami with the artisan's skillful maneuver. The needle shone in the sunshine and the workman's dynamic arm moved rhythmically.

There were also a few parks in the neighborhood, with swings and a teeter totter and children gathered there to play. We were told by our mother that we should never stay there until it got dark, we should never stay there if we were alone and we should never give out our name or address to strangers.

Once I was on a swing and was swinging happily. There were several adults, standing around and one of the men asked me what my name was. My sisters and I were good-looking children and since we were tall, especially I, because of the Korean blood, a lot of people mistook me for much older. So I was quite used to men showing interest in me and knew how to handle it. I said to myself: "Here it comes", but I pretended to be an innocent child. I answered: "Kazuko"-a totally false name.

"Where do you live?" the man asked me.

"I live in the huge house at the corner—you know. We have five maids: two chambermaids and three for general use."

I swung as high as I could, laughing. The man sensed I was kidding and fell silent. In fact, he was a decent-looking fellow. He may have been just curious to find out those things without any malicious intention. At the sound of "five maids", he knew I was kidding him. Even though it was the era of hiring maids, in a normal household, three would be the limit. I soon got off the swing and headed home feeling rather pleased that I had tricked a grown man. I was only nine years old.

There was also a stream nearby where we went to catch tadpoles. We wore rubber boots and took a small bucket and a small ladle net. We slid down the bank of the stream and waded into the water. Catching tadpoles was a seasonal game. If one missed the timing, there would be no tadpoles; they had all turned into frogs. The frogs that were fortunate enough to escape our invasion, hopped around in abundance in the fields nearby.

We also went to catch cicadas, butterflies and dragonflies. In the middle of summer, most cicadas were brown. Towards the end of the summer and the beginning of autumn, there were ming-ming cicadas. They were commonly called by that name because their cry sounded like "min—g, min—g". Their bodies were smaller and their wings were transparent. My mother, who was anxious to make me healthy and strong, put a hat on my head and a net in my hand and encouraged me to go out and catch the insects. The school also required samples of insects for a summer assignment.

It was tricky to catch a cicada. One got some resin from a pine tree and after kneading it between two fingers, smeared it at the end of a long stick. Stealthily on tiptoes, with this stick poised, one approached a cicada. Sometimes a cicada was positioned out of reach but some had the misfortune of staying too low. But some of them were sensitive enough to feel the danger and flew away. Only a few had the bad luck of being caught by me, who was not particularly clever at these things.

Looking back, I feel sorry for cicadas, butterflies and other insects that got caught, drugged, killed and pinned in a box to become samples. Grasshoppers and crickets were kept in a cage and released after a few days but I don't think they enjoyed their captivity for any length of time.

In spring, the field was covered with horsetails. They seemed to stick their heads out of the ground almost instantly. Once, I went to our usual open field playground. The horsetails looked enticing. I picked a few and went to the edge of the field and looked down. Some feet below, there was another patch of vacant land, carpeted with green grass. I thought I would jump down. I jumped. I did land on my feet but a dull pain stabbed straight up from the soles of my feet to my head through my spine like a blunt rod. Then I knew I had done something very dangerous and I was lucky not to have been seriously hurt. I miscalculated the distance. It was much too far for jumping down.

chapter VI

Although I got along well with everyone in class, I never had a so-called bosom friend. I noticed that my classmates formed little groups to which they belonged or chose one particular person with whom they did everything together. I. used to wonder why, as I never felt the need to attach myself to another person to the extent that I would go to the toilet with her. I was too independent. In those days, women were expected to be subservient, not to have any opinions, not to be independent and not to waste time on reading or to want to have a higher education. I hated the so-called feminine demeanor that was merely superficially nice. Under this cover, women were crafty and mean. Because of my Korean blood, I was too open and vulnerable and could not cope with the Japanese temperament. Not only the difference in blood, but also the fact that I read a lot, isolated me from other girls just like a drop of oil in water can never be mixed. My vast reading gave me a far more advanced knowledge about life and the world and separated me and the other girls into two different worlds. There was no common subject I could talk about with the others. I was reading world history in classic Japanese while the others hardly opened a book that started with "Once upon a time."

Being half Korean, I was not naive to believe that Japanese soldiers were fighting in China for a just cause. I was wide awake to the world situation and social injustices. I was keenly aware of racial prejudices. Everyday, we lived in fear that someone would find out that we were

Koreans and might insult us. Every time I had to give my name to a stranger, I had a little pang in my heart. On hearing my Korean name, people invariably looked surprised. "Are you Korean?" The question was followed by: "But you don't look it." I laughed to myself at their ignorance. The Japanese knew only the Koreans, who worked at the jobs the Japanese shunned since they were not given opportunities to better themselves. These Koreans had to immigrate to Japan because they lost their country when it was subjugated by Japan.

But I did not tell my mother about these things. I somehow sensed that she was a nice woman but did not have the spiritual depth to comprehend philosophical concepts. After all, she was pure Japanese and did not understand what a mixed-race child felt and thought. The insults inflicted on her hit her harder than they did me because she was insulted for what she wasn't. Her way of coping with the prejudice was to make efforts to eliminate everything Korean and be as Japanese as possible. But I didn't want to be Japanese. That's not what I was. Equally, I did not want to be Korean, either. Pure-blooded people never understood that. Later my mother broadened her perspective, mainly through my influence. When I was insulted, I handled them quietly, in my own way and nursed the hurts by myself. One thing I detested more than open insults was fake attempts for understanding. The Japanese who tried to be friendly in a condescending manner were the worst. I preferred insults. At least they were honest.

My elder sister could not cope with anything by herself.

"So and so called me Korean", "So and so said my name was funny," she had to tell my mother, who always got worked up. I wondered why she could not keep it to herself and resolve the problem in silence. There are many types of prejudices in this world. If one gets hung up on one subject, life can be pretty miserable. Ours just happened to be our being Korean. Unlike me, who had to eat lunch by myself when we went on school excursions because I did not belong to any group and did not begrudge it, she needed someone she could glue herself to.

In her class, there was a girl by the name of Satoko. She had an elder sister who was not particularly brilliant but Satoko excelled in school and was always at the top of her class. Their mother was a widow. Her husband was an army officer who died young. Once, I saw his photo which was placed in a "butsudan" (an altar for ancestor worship). It showed a nice-looking military officer in his uniform with a long saber in his hand.

In those days, any widowed woman had a hard time earning a living. Satoko's mother ran a boarding house for young male students. This was more than a bed and breakfast as dinner had to be made and there was the added problem of having to deal with young men with raging testosterone. The problem was doubled when there were two pre-teen girls living under the same roof. With only a few opportunities available for young fellows to get to know women, the first targets would be the landlady's daughters.

The mother, with a small pension from the army for her deceased husband and the income from running the boarding house, still had difficulty making ends meet. Whether she had her own physical need or not, I do not know, but she became the mistress of a man who came to visit her regularly. Once, I saw him enter a room in their house during the daytime. He was a typical middle-aged Japanese fellow. He was stout and of middle height and he did not smile at anyone. He wore a dark mantle over a kimono.

As the girls were getting on to puberty and becoming aware of sexuality, Satoko started sensing why this man came to visit her mother from time to time. She became moody and took out her frustrations on anyone weaker than herself. My elder sister was a good target. She couldn't do anything without this girl, who had a mean streak in her character.

One of the reasons why my sister needed to lean on someone constantly was that she did not excel in intellectual subjects, although she was much better than I was in subjects like sewing, crafts and gymnastics. Her place in her class was always a little over the middle. But it is excelling in intellectual subjects that wins the respect of others and leads to independence and self-respect.

My sister once came home and wailed to our mother: "Satoko said, 'Oh, your name is Boku? All Koreans seem to have names like Kim and Boku'." Satoko wanted to rub in the fact that my sister was Korean and my sister was hurt. In fact, the statement was correct since as there are only about one hundred surnames in Korea; one is bound to be Kim, Park

(Boku), Chang or Yun and so forth. At the time "Kims" and "Bokus" seemed to be overflowing in Japan. My sister simply did not have the wit or guts to retort by saying: "A lot of Japanese names seem to be Tanaka, Suzuki or Watanabe and such."

The big grudge I had over my sister's friendship with Satoko was that it rippled over to me. My mother did not understand that the year and a half age difference between my sister and me played a big role. We did not have the same life style. My sister's dependence on Satoko, who was obviously playing with psychological warfare, irritated me to no end.

Every morning, we walked to school. My sister and I left home early enough so that we could get to school on time. Unfortunately, Satoko's house was on the way. Her mother asked us to stop by so that we three could go to school together. For what purpose, I don't know. Since I was always independent, I never understood why Satoko could not go to school by herself. So we stopped at her house. Her mother made us wait in her little shop, the front of her house which she had converted into a shop of notions to supplement her income. Since she had not the means to pay for a lot for supplies, the selection was poor and she had few clients. I could see the stock sitting in the shop, was only collecting dust and Lilian embroidery (a fashionable craft at the time) thread was fading on a display fixture in the strong sunshine coming from the west. I felt an acute sense of her business failure.

There were also several cheap metal belts lying in a display case. At home, my elder sister insisted on buying one of them and my mother had a hard time trying to dissuade her from doing so. She told her that such a cheap item would not suit her. Those belts were also unsold.

While I was staring at those symbols of a failed venture, Satoko was getting ready for school. She was never ready when we arrived. I think she was taking her time on purpose to annoy us. Her mother was scuffling back and forth between the shop and the interior of the house, apologizing to us. I used to think: "If you are worried, why don't you kick her ass." Because of the time wasted, we had to hurry to school because Satoko would appear only when there was just enough time to rush to school. I hated these kinds of typical Japanese feminine tricks and despised my sister for not being able to stand up for herself. I think my mother finally intervened when she learned that we were nearly late for school everyday due to Satoko's daily exercise. After a while, we went to school straight from home.

One event concerning Satoko's tricks stands out in my memory as vivid as a memorable motion picture. There was in the neighborhood, a branch school of a famous Protestant school, called Aoyama Gakuin. Every school, including the school I attended, had a drama day. Aoyama Gakuin, being a private school with a higher standard for dramas, had an open house and put on a play. I went to the theatre (they even had a proper theatre) early and saved three seats right in front of the stage. About five minutes before the curtain, I saw my sister at the door, waving at me. She came over and said that Satoko had saved seats in a better location. I was naive enough to believe it. So I abandoned the nice front seats and went to the door. Of course she had done none of the sort and I missed the whole play.

I did not like girls, especially Japanese girls. They had no opinion of their own and yet were full of insidious tricks. If I didn't like them, they didn't like me either. But I got along well with boys. When I was in Grade Five, I was elected as a vice-president of the class. Each class held an election each semester and chose one president and two vice-presidents and I was chosen as one of the vice-presidents. At around this time, the school was renovating a part of the building and our grade was squeezed into a corner with a thin partition wall separating two classes. Behind the thin wall was an all-boy class. The president of the boys' class was a decent looking boy with a little more class than the others. He was neatly dressed and looked quite intelligent. He also had a physical handicap. His neck was slanted to one side so he could not hold his head straight.

I think I got to know him when the presidents of the two classes had to get together to discuss some issues. These were the days when men and women did not talk to one another; let alone little boys and girls. As usual, I defied the rules. During recess I spoke to him. He was delighted. He liked me and called me by my first name. His neck did not bother me. He looked nice and I could tell that he came from a nice family. He obviously appreciated my attention. He must have had an inferiority complex about his neck and my ignoring it must have pleased him. He must also have disliked his macho classmates because he was more delicate and sensitive.

When I left the classroom for recess, I looked around for him and if he was not out yet, I would wait for him and he did the same. Then we talked. Since the partition wall was thin, sometimes we could hear the boys' voices from the next room. One day, I heard his voice. It must have been the composition class and he must have written the best composition. He was reading it out loud to his class. I could hear his clear intelligent voice and I was listening to it with my whole body. I was in love with this boy.

One day, we were talking and laughing as usual during recess. Some of his classmates took notice of us. A group of bullies came over and sneered at him: "Hey, you are talking to a woman?" My friend immediately turned pale and speechless. Rage gripped me. I could tell that he was used to shrivelling up at every insult because of his handicap. He just could not stand up to any physical or emotional assault. In an instant, I could feel all the insults and hurts he must have endured because of his neck. One look at his face gave me that insight.

I wanted to protect him. Without thinking, I slapped the bully's face with all the strength I could muster.

Deep silence fell. I was immediately remorseful. I said to myself: "What have I done?" and was sorry that my Korean temperament made me lose my temper so easily. Since he was the worst bully in his class, I was sure he would hit me back and I would be in a big trouble. He didn't. He must have been too stunned to have any kind of reaction. He obviously had never witnessed a woman speak up against a man or see a woman raise her hand against a man. Since the experience was so totally new, he probably didn't know how to react. He just stood there in silence. Everybody else stood there in silence. To break this awkward situation, the bell rang and we all trailed back into the classrooms.

Shortly before the end of the semester, my love came over to me and said in a low voice: "Misao-chan, I must say goodbye to you. I am going to have surgery on my neck and after that I am going to a private school. So next semester I shall not be here."

I was glad that he was going to have his neck corrected (I did not

Aiko's Journey

know if the surgery would be successful) and get out of the rough atmosphere of the public school but my heart was sad. His last "Sayonara" still rings in my ears.

At around the same time, I got to know another boy. His name was Kono. I don't know how I got to know him since he did not attend the same school as I did. I still can see him coming around the corner of the street with a hand-knitted beige sweater on and with magazines under his arm to lend them to me. His long legs and knees stuck out of blue short pants. In those days, all young boys wore short pants. It was a great occasion when they graduated to long trousers.

He was so anxious to please me. He was an only child and like my departed love, he could not handle rough boys. Neither of the two boys I knew, would have gotten along well with other Japanese girls either. They would have been too conscious of their gender. He proudly took me to his house and introduced me to his mother. He lived in one of the newly developed middle-class houses. I could sense that the family was not overly well off but comfortably off and the father had a steady income.

His mother, dressed in a kimono and a typical Japanese housewives' "kappogi" (an apron that covers the whole front and the sleeves of a kimono), came rushing out and bowed to me several times.

"Thank you, thank you. You see, my boy has no friends. Please, be my boy's friend. Thank you for being my boy's friend."

I felt like a benevolent queen. Kono watched both of us with a contented look. He took me to his room where he had books lined up on bookshelves.

"I never lend my books to anyone, but to you, I will lend any books. Which ones do you want to take?"

I simply pointed out a few books and out they came from the bookshelves. He subscribed to a magazine that came out once a month, a very reasonable magazine for children by a famous publishing company, called Kodansha. Only this magazine cost 50sen. My mother refused to pay 50sen for a magazine I would have finished reading in thirty minutes. Kono would lend me his magazine even before he had read it himself. Thus I accumulated knowledge and learned a lot at someone else's expense.

But our friendship was terminated soon. When my mother saw our friendship blossoming, she asked me: "Does his mother know that you are half Korean?"

"I don't think so."

I didn't think I had told Kono my last name. I didn't think Kono's mother even suspected that.

"You'd better stop seeing him then," my mother said, "before his mother finds out and changes her attitude abruptly."

I reluctantly obeyed. I, myself, would have continued visiting him until the day his mother changed her attitude, if she ever did. I am quite sure Kono would have liked me even then. If his mother had forced him to put a stop to our friendship, he would have complained. I WAS skeptical of his mother, though. She didn't look like the kind of person who had enough intellectual resources not to have racial prejudices. She was quite ordinary. So maybe my mother was right.

My mother bought me, once in a while, second-hand books at a night market. I forgot how often it came round, perhaps once a month. Booths of various stores lined the street. Acetylene gas was burned to light the booths. They carried various wares: kitchen utensils, second-hand kimonos, shoes, small Japanese ornaments for women, plants and books. I would be glued to the book booth, leafing through the books cautiously and my mother had to loosen her purse strings. Since they were second hand, the books were cheap. They cost only five or ten sen. Even then, it was an extra expense. I still remember the happy feeling of walking around with my parents and my sisters under the dark summer sky going from one booth to another. It was late when we got home.

There was also a yearly summer festival at the parish shrine. Men from the neighborhood practiced "taiko" (drumming) and women rehearsed for a performance on the stage. The booths similar to those at a night market, displayed their wares: cotton candy, brown syrup candy, cheap toys that didn't last long, games and paper crafts. They sold big dolls for 50 sen but it was too much money for us since my sister and I each only got 10 sen to spend. So we bought ground cherries.

We had to be careful to buy the ones that were the right ripeness. If they were too green, they would break in the process of squeezing out the inside. If they were of just the right ripeness, we gently coaxed out the inside by softly squeezing the sides with two fingers. When we successfully squeezed out the inside without breaking it, we washed it with water, put it in our mouths, and maneuvered it to make noise. This was called "Hoozuki".

The people of the community decorated the open space in front of the shrine with gaudy colours. The men would go out with the "omikoshi" (the portable shrine) into the street with shouts of "Essa, essa" and other words. They would push and pull while some men cheered them on. They tried to arouse more excitement by waving a big "uchiwa" (flat fan).

One summer, my elder sister and I went to the shrine early. My father said that he would join us later with my younger sister. They arrived. My young father, wearing a "yukata" (a cotton kimono) and holding the plump hand of my younger sister, walked towards us. Keiko's other hand was holding a stick of a brown syrup candy, which my father had been telling us over the years not to buy. He used to scold us severely when we suggested that we buy it.

My heart was stung with jealousy and annoyed with my father's inconsistency. This was the beginning of my parents' spoiling Keiko and it started driving a wedge between us sisters. I think my parents could not really enjoy their first two children, though they did love us, because they were financially not well off when we were growing up. By the time Keiko was about three or four years old, the financial situation was more settled and they had enough time to enjoy her. My parents must have experienced a sort of "empty nest syndrome" since the older ones were growing up and having their own lives. They found a nice object in my younger sister to occupy themselves with.

As the situation with the war worsened, all the festivities and pleasures of life disappeared.

chapter VII

We moved to another rented house. It was situated at the corner of a crossroads. In the direction towards the school, there was a slight hill. At the bottom of the hill, there was a cluster of little shops: a "sakaya" (shop that sold sake, soy sauce, salt and spices), a shoe repair shop, a pharmacy and a little bake shop with a space for a few tables and chairs. "Sakaya" was the only shop in the neighborhood with a new invention called the telephone. But in those days, the connection was often bad and speaking on the phone was stressful. One day, I was ordered by my mother to use this phone to deliver a message to someone and I was very nervous. My mother, whenever she felt timid about mentioning her Korean name, often sent me, a mere child, out on the mission.

The little bake shop was run by a woman and her daughter who had a child. The daughter must have been divorced or must have had an illegitimate child. I could sense that they had some problems. Their unenthusiastic attitude about the business and lack of funds were obvious in the scantiness of the wares. But sometimes I bought a Danish there to take it to school for my lunch.

We would pack our lunches, which consisted of rice and side dishes such as, a scrap of fish, omelet and red pickled ginger, in a little metal container. There were special lunch boxes sold for this purpose. Some of the lunch boxes had pretty patterns on the lid. During the winter, each classroom had a wood-burning stove at the front of the classroom and over it, there was a modified oven with shelves inside where the children could leave their lunchboxes in the morning so that the lunch would be warm at noon. If one had not left the lunchbox in the right spot it would not heat up properly. Some girls were aggressive in securing a good spot but I was not. My rice was often partially cold.

Although I ritually left my lunchbox there in the morning, when lunch break came around, I barely ate it. I could not stand the smell of the soy sauce, seaweed, fish and other foods hitting my face as we opened the oven. I opened the lid of the lunchbox and shut it almost immediately. So my mother gave me some money to buy a Danish. Even then, I left it uneaten. I did not like the atmosphere in school. I could not consume food unless the surroundings were nice. When the War got worse and we had almost nothing to eat, I was sorry that I had not eaten my lunch. I was not the only one who regretted disrespecting lunch. One famous novelist wrote after the War that he was sorry for throwing away his perfectly good lunch in days of peace time.

The house we rented was bigger and had a second floor. From one of the windows upstairs, we could see Mount Fuji on a clear day. There were three rooms downstairs and two rooms upstairs. The main bedroom downstairs had eight tatami mats. It faced a tiny little yard that the Japanese say is "as small as a cat's forehead." Since the bedroom faced north, it was always semi-dark and no sunshine ever visited the room. My mother found out that a sick person lay in this room for years and was horrified. But we stayed. The rent was fifty yen.

As usual, each month, my mother sent me to the landlord's house to pay the rent. The landlord used to be a genteel land owner in the area and lived in a big strong farm house several blocks away. The rumour was that the family had leprosy running in their blood and their babies were born without hair. Since I was pathologically frightened of leprosy, I hesitated to touch the door to open it. I was afraid that I might catch the disease. But I can't remember washing my hands afterwards. Maybe I was just afraid theoretically.

We were financially better off because my father landed a job with the North China Development Company. Soon afterwards, my parents made a great sacrifice for us children. My father was keen on sending us to a private Christian school. He particularly liked the Christian teaching that all men are equal. In the teachings of Christ, children would not suffer racial discrimination. But in order to earn enough money to pay the tuition of a private school, he decided to go and work in China. This would give him a higher wage. It also meant a separation from the family and a lonely bachelor life for him.

Shortly before his departure, I went upstairs and caught him looking out a window. He was wearing a cotton kimono. His shoulders told me he was thinking of the life to come. Various thoughts must have been racing in his mind. He sensed that I was standing in silence; he turned and smiled at me. How I loved my father! How grateful I am now to my parents!

My father loved his family so much that he came home from China every six months. As soon as he had saved enough money, he would hop on a train and come home with suitcases full of souvenirs. We would go and meet him at the train station. When we saw him, we hailed. I can't remember how we carried his suitcases because I can't remember taking taxis. Maybe we walked, carrying the suitcases among us. Opening the suitcases was a joyful celebration. They contained so many exotic items that it was like opening a door to a new world. A Chinese doll, a European-made wrist watch (this was for my mother), a Chinese lampshade, a rose stone necklace and an exquisitely embroidered cloth. We gawked, sighed and made cries of awe as each item was taken out of the suitcases. Eventually, we even got a teak table with an inlay; this, he must have sent through mail.

We finally could afford holidays. We went to Haruna Lake and Hakone and Atami. We went to Haruna during the summer. We rented a row boat and my father rowed. I have a picture of us sitting in the little boat and even in the photograph (black and white), my face looks sun tanned.

We went to Hakone during the winter. We meant to stay at Hakone Mountain but when we went to a Japanese inn, the place was crowded and did not look nice at all. So my father decided we would walk to Atami, which was quite a distance from the top of the mountain. The children in Japan, in those days, were not spoiled so Sakae and I had no trouble. My father carried Keiko on his back and my mother in her kimono strove to walk. I still have the vision of my mother swaying her hips in order to catch up with us. It was late afternoon when we arrived in Atami. We chose a decent-looking Japanese inn and spent the night there. When I woke next morning, I saw white powder gently falling from the half-dark sky.

There was another thing that appeared in our household that was supposed to be a luxury item. It was a small harmonium. In those days, when it took over a month on a ship to get to Europe and from two to three weeks to sail to the U.S.A., everything Western was a luxury item. Only moneyed families could afford pianos or any other foreign musical instruments. The harmonium was the beginning of our ownership of foreign musical instruments. The smallest harmonium had only a limited number of keys. It needed to be upgraded to a larger one, step by step, until one possessed a reasonably proper harmonium with enough stops. My mother, who had absolutely no knowledge of Western music, had acquired bits of information here and there, acted on her discretion and bought the smallest harmonium. This was the first keyboard instrument I ever touched.

As my father was absent for months in China, my mother befriended the teacher, who was a male, of my class. He was engaged to a young woman who was in his home city, Osaka. Being a bachelor, he was bored and gladly accepted my mother's invitation to dinner. After school, I went home first and changed into a better dress and went back to school to fetch him. My mother put a wine-coloured bow in my hair to make it a special occasion.

Now, Mr. Nasumoto, our new teacher, was a special addition to our school. He graduated from the Imperial University (now Tokyo University) with a B.A. degree. It was an unprecedented honour in a public elementary school to have a teacher with a degree from the Imperial University. I noticed that his method of teaching, since he did not go to the teachers' college, lacked the certain skill of other teachers but he taught me a way to look at things. He taught me how to think.

For instance, he told us the story about a village where only one man in the whole village knew that the next rainfall would make everyone insane. He, therefore, warned all the villagers not to get wet from this rainfall but the others did not believe him and laughed at him. The rain came and the man shut himself in his house, whereas all the others got wet. Consequently, they all went insane. The man who escaped the madness was now considered to be insane by all the others.

He also was aware of what was going on in the world. He bemoaned the fact that Japan was considered to be a primitive country by whites. He said that the Western world did not even know that Japan possessed a well-developed railway system, radio or any other modern inventions. I don't think such matters even bothered other teachers' minds.

As I went to fetch Mr. Nasumoto, I was tickled with pleasure and honour that my teacher would come to our house. After dinner, we children were sent to bed upstairs. I strained my ears to listen to the grown-ups' conversation downstairs. Although I knew a bit about male-female relationships from reading adult books, it never occurred to me that my mother would be unfaithful to my father. My mother got a handful of gossip from Mr. Nasumoto and told us later. When I come to think of it now, it was not such an advisable thing to do, but neither my sister nor I ever leaked it at school or told anybody else. My elder sister, who was less mature in such matters and had a not-so-strong memory, must have forgotten as soon as she heard it.

But I knew that Nasumoto was currently having an affair with a married woman whose husband was also away for work. The lady was an ardent fan of "Takarazuka", all female theatre, and although she was middle-aged (thirty-five years old), she would frequent the show and scream at her favorite stars unabashedly. Her husband was beginning to suspect the situation and talk of divorce was in the offing. Mr. Nasumoto wanted to extricate himself from occupying the empty side of her bed.

He had also gotten engaged recently and wanted to make his future bride happy as he could foresee that she would have a pretty difficult time after the marriage. The lot of an ordinary housewife in those days was not easy. The washing had to be done by hand and the kitchen was inconvenient. When children arrived, the woman's work became even more frantic. So a fresh young girl at the time of the marriage turned into a tired middle-aged looking housewife within the year. In addition to all the problems, the young woman had to live with the in-laws and often there was no such thing as a sweet honeymoon.

Mr. Nasumoto had a widowed mother who had worked hard to put him through university. She was going to live with the young couple after their marriage. So he was working hard to give his fiancée a nice memory upon which she could look back and draw energy for when the hard times came. Since it was not a love marriage, he wanted to cultivate in her some romantic feelings. So he was writing love letters to her and they seemed to have some effect. I was impressed by his wisdom. Here was a truly clever man.

He imparted his wisdom to my mother. He would never marry a woman from Tokyo, he said, as the temperaments of the two cities are too different. One must marry someone from the same area. He would never think of marrying a girl who was half Korean. This made my mother sad but I thought she was silly. The feelings were mutual. I would never have married a Japanese man. As much as I admired the wisdom of Mr. Nasumoto, I could never imagine myself as his wife. I was not going to give up the opportunity for a higher education, to read, and to better myself. I knew even then that the world was wide and I did not have to worry if a Japanese man did not want to marry me.

Mr. Nasumoto, with equal patience and gentleness, opened my mother's eyes to foreign literature. My father sent us orders for books but his choice of books was different from that of Mr. Nasumoto's. My father tended to be more academic, and included Shakespeare and political satire about Russian communism, "Golden Calf" but these were above my mother's appreciation. My father did not like novels. With Mr. Nasumoto's guidance, soon the bookshelves started filling up with novels such as "Pierre et Jean", "Une Vie" by Maupassant and other French novelists. I think Tolstoy's "Anna Karenina" got to the bookshelf during this period. I don't think my mother really appreciated French novels but I did. Government censorship crossed out the lines on a page with any description of physical love or anything that faintly suggested it. Sometimes more than half of a page was filled with dots. I used to stare at the dots that filled the space, trying to guess what must have been written there but I understood vaguely what was described beyond the space.

There was another male teacher who was of a new breed. He was far more modern and sophisticated. He was a dandy and paid more attention to his appearance. He was extremely popular among the girls in the higher grades since the girls were awakening to puberty and were susceptible to male attraction.

Once he ran around the school yard for the purpose of exercise and I saw a group of girls running after him with their cheeks flushed. I never joined his club. I despised the shallowness of the groupies. I never had a yen for superficially handsome fellows. Mr. Ono found out that Mr. Nasumoto was a frequent guest for dinners at our house. He wanted to get on the wagon. He came and taught my sister how to play the harmonium. His knowledge of playing was pretty superficial but skillful. He then taught us about popular Italian songs such as "0, Sole Mio" and "Come Back to Sorrento." Mr. Nasumoto may have possessed a B.A. from the Imperial University but he was brought up by a widowed mother who earned a living by peddling kimonos and was no match when it came to popularity. Mr. Ono was a flamboyant dashing knight in aluminum armour.

Mr. Ono was also having an affair with a married woman at whose house he was lodging. At the time we got to know him, he had just left this place, and did not know what to do with his belongings. He begged my mother to keep them in our house for a while. So one day, piles of cardboard boxes containing his suits arrived, together with a violin in a case. They went upstairs and sat in a corner of the bedroom. The strings of the violin were broken from disuse.

In Japan, suits or dresses do not hang in a wardrobe because the structure of the house needs open space. The suits and dresses are put away after each season in boxes with mothballs. When the season comes, the suits or dresses are taken out of the boxes and ironed for use. Mr. Ono's suits were neatly folded and placed in boxes—twenty-four of them! The number overwhelmed us.

My father possessed two suits for each season. He did not even allow for the subtle difference between the beginning of summer and full summer. He never worried how he looked as long as he was clean and decent looking. Yet, he was very handsome. He would not even imagine using fragrance to entice the opposite sex. I thought this was the way all men were. Mr. Ono belonged to a different world. I discovered for the first time that even men paid attention to their looks and worried about what to wear.

Mr. Ono did all kinds of things skillfully. He was a window looking out to a different landscape. Even at school, he put on an entirely different play on Drama Day. Once a year, the teacher trained his or her class to perform on the stage. All the other classes put on some conservative, traditional children's plays but he had trained his class to perform a musical. He put some of his male students (he had an all-male class) in girls' outfits and let them sing and dance. He astonished and charmed the whole school, much to the chagrin of the other teachers. I think he WAS musical.

I don't think my mother really sat down and talked to him the same way she did with Mr. Nasumoto because Mr. Ono was busy trying his charms elsewhere. Actually, he was engaged. He showed his fidelity to this one woman he loved by never kissing the women he slept with. Kissing was the privilege reserved for this one and only woman.

The neighbours gossiped about the comings and goings of these men but when my father came home, he met with them. He wrote a letter from China to my mother telling her to be careful because: "Love had no shape and cannot be proven." I never doubted my mother's fidelity. My instinct told me that she was not doing anything wrong.

My elder sister was preparing for the entrance examination into the "joggakko" (girls school). When one got to Grade Six, the class was divided into two groups. One group consisted of the students who were going to "joggakko" and the other of the students who went to commercial high schools. Those, who did neither, finished schooling after Grade Six or went to school for one more year. "Joggakko" was for five years and commercial schools were for four years. But the true distinction was the cold hard class distinction. "Joggakko" was for better class children and those who went to commercial schools would be prepared for work.

In the days when working women were looked down upon and treated shabbily, this was the first taste of reality for the girls whose family was either not educated enough or moneyed enough. Since commercial schools needed no preparation for entry, the girls were dismissed when the school day ended at around three. Those who were considered to be privileged stayed on to be drilled in the subjects that would appear on the examination. The extracurricular classes lasted for hours. Sometimes my sister came home when the day was waning into darkness. This extra load of work had an affect on her health. She was diagnosed with "rikumaku". She had to stay home to just rest and after a few weeks, when she returned to school, she no longer studied so rigorously.

Then there was the problem of choosing a school. My father was not in Japan. So the task of deciding which school to choose fell upon my mother's shoulders. The first choice for Sakae was Aoyama Gakuin, a famous Protestant Christian school, the auditorium of which I had to leave because of Satoko's nasty tricks. Since the selection by the school would be made by examining the transcript, a written examination and a personal interview, one should not aspire to go to a school out of one's range. My mother did not know much about modern Christian schools, so she asked a Keisen student's mother and also Miss Sasaki who was our previous neighbour and happened to be teaching English grammar at Keisen. Weighing all matters and upon the advice of the teacher, my mother changed to Keisen.

Keisen was founded by a woman by the name of Michi Kawai. She studied at Tsuda Women's College and went to the U.S.A. to further her studies. When she established the school, she was about forty-two years old. Her school began in a private house with a handful of students. It soon grew. By the time my sister entered it, it had grown to be a full-sized school, although the size of each class was still small. The school had moved to a suburb of Tokyo and from the nearest station, Kyodo, it was about a twenty- minute walk.

Keisen turned out to be a very good school. Miss K, the principal had a unique philosophy and the school taught about God. They had worship every morning and there were constant prayer meetings. On the first day of school, my sister brought back pretty little gadgets that had an air of culture and high class. A little box, covered with remnants of Japanese fabrics, was for discarded needles. Book covers were made of flowery feminine looking materials. Those pretty little things were the doors that opened up a new world to more refinement. The girls in the upper grades guided and taught the newcomers with kindness.

In the meantime I was left alone, so I played with Keiko. Sakae grew emotionally in the normal way. When she entered into puberty, she lost interest in playing with dolls. She and I each had a special porcelain doll. They were usually kept in a glass case and we were allowed to play with them only on special occasions. But Sakae no longer enjoyed playing with hers. My younger sister was at the stage when she touched everything, so she opened the case, took the dolls out and messed them up. Since Sakae had no more interest, she did not mind it. But I did mind. I did not become a woman in the same way Sakae did. A part of me was always a child. I would always cherish my doll. My heart makes me love it regardless of my age. A beautiful doll always speaks to me. I did not grow up as the years passed away. My mother did not understand me. My mother could not understand why a big girl like me still clung to the doll. I watched my doll get destroyed and a part of me was torn away. My heart was sadder because my mother did not protect me.

Since I remained partly a child, it did not bother me to play with Keiko who was six years younger than I. We rode her tricycle. Since I was tall and my legs were too long, I stuck them out sideways. We slid down the hill over and over again. I still hear the ring of my sister's happy laughter. Again, my mother thought this was mighty peculiar coming from a girl six years older than her sister. She laughed. There were many things my mother did not understand.

Around this time, the great novel "Gone with the Wind" hit the shores of Japan. Up to this point, we were not well acquainted with American literature. But the introduction of "Gone with the Wind" opened our eyes to the U.S. of America which was ranked lower than Europe. Regardless of the worsening relationship between the U.S.A. and Japan, the book's translator, Yasuo Okubo and the author, Margaret Mitchell, were exchanging amiable letters.

Since every translation in Japanese becomes much longer than the original, it came out in four volumes. My elder sister and I were fascinated by the life of the Southern belles and fought for the right to read it first. My sister who was stubborn, insisted on the first right and I was annoyed. She was a slow reader so it would take too long before my turn came. At one point we decided to read it together, she from the right side and I from the left side. I discovered that I could read five pages while she was trying to finish one page. So I finally gave up and gave her the first volume and started reading the second volume. But every time she put down the book, I picked it up and read. I finished it completely before she did and I went on to the second volume in peace.

We tried to be ladies according to the examples shown in the book and giggled at our own efforts. We were totally attracted to Rhett Butler. We would never have declared the Pacific War. Anybody who read this book and declared war would have to be a complete idiot. War means disaster as described in this book and not a party where young men want to show off their prowess. The militaristic government that declared war on the U.S.A. later was, therefore, less intelligent than I who was only eleven years old.

When my sister went to joggakko, she latched herself onto two other classmates. One was Kiyoko and the other Harumi. Kiyoko had lost her father so she, her elder brother and their mother were living with their paternal grandfather, who was a member of the House of Peers. The House of Peers mainly consisted of the members of the nobility but also allowed in a few commoners who paid a large amount of taxes. Their grandfather was one of the latter and was well off enough to look after his son's entire family.

Kiyoko complained to Harumi and my sister: "My grandfather said he wanted to give us a gift. He placed the present behind him and gave us a long lecture on how precious this thing was, how fortunate we were to receive it and went on and on. I wanted to scream, 'Do you want to give it or not? If you do, just get on with it. Just simply give it to us'"

Kiyoko's older brother was a student at the Imperial University. One great advantage of getting to know someone whose brother was going to university, especially one of a high ranking, is that they had books. University students in those days were elite intellectuals and they were at the stage where they started pondering political, philosophical, social and sexual issues. They were on the threshold of finding out about life and sexuality.

One day, Sakae came home grinning. She whispered to me: "I have a book I want to show you. Don't tell mother." So we sneaked upstairs. She took a book out of her school bag. I gasped at the title of the book. It was called "Market of Kisses." She borrowed it from Kiyoko whose brother purchased it. Some publishers were always attempting to publish erotic books to make money. They quickly published such books and equally swiftly sold them to the readers known to them. The business was conducted mostly underground. They tried to sell as many books as possible before the officials of the censorship board came down upon them with an order of prohibition. The originals of such books were uncensored and, therefore, every word was printed.

My sister and I made a pact that each of us would go downstairs to help our mother if she needed help while the other would read the book. Since it was she who borrowed the book, she would get to read it first. My mother called so I went downstairs. Not only was my heart on the book which was about to disclose the secrets between men and women, I was also totally inefficient in housekeeping matters.

My mother soon lost patience. "Oh, you are no help at all," she said, "get your sister." I went upstairs gleefully.

"Mother wants you. Not me." She put the book down and went downstairs reluctantly. She unfortunately proved herself to be helpful so she was not released for a long time, giving me ample time to finish the book without interruption.

The book was about a heroine by the name of Midori who took on a younger lover. She was one of the so-called "bad girls." She would be a model of chastity according to the standard of the 1990s but in the 1930s, she was an example of immorality. There was a section in the book which described a man and a woman engaged in actual love-making and paid guests would peep from the next room through the gap in the sliding doors, purposefully left ajar. In the end, Midori's young lover died of consumption and she left for Europe to console herself. In those days consumption was a convenient solution for ending many romances beautifully.

Keiko was growing up to be a pretty little girl. Not only was she far apart from us in age, she was quite different temperamentally. I think she was the normal one and I was different. I didn't care for playing with other children as much as she did. If anything, I didn't want to play with them. Since I had read so many adult books, I could not stand other children who were still reading: "Once upon a time..." Some of them did not even read. I had no common interests with other children to talk about and I was not particularly interested in playing games.

But Keiko wanted to play. Since there was no playmate in the family, she went on an expedition and got to know the Isobe household where there were plenty of children to play with. In that family, there were about five children. The youngest was an infant and still breast-feeding. I didn't know what kind of occupation the husband had but it certainly was a solid middle-class family. The children were not well behaved. Mrs. Isobe was obviously too tired from producing babies constantly to teach manners to her children. She neither had energy nor the time to do that. She let everything run its course. She was the kind of woman who reminded me of lukewarm flannel night-gowns. For feeding purposes, the front of her kimono was almost always sloppily half open and her baby hung from her breast like a limp lump.

Mrs. Isobe's younger brother was staying with the family while he was going to university. Obviously he had to make himself useful in order to make up for his free stay. He would go to a tofu shop with a metal container in hand. These were the days when no decent male would be caught seen with a shopping package in hand. He was a laughing stock in the neighbourhood but he persevered.

My mother did not approve of Keiko's going over there and making friends with the Isobes. She never knew how to handle people so when Mrs. Isobe, who had too much time on her hands despite her many children, descended upon my mother, she did not know how to repel the unwanted visit. Trailing behind Mrs. Isobe came all her other children who could walk. The soles of their feet were dirty and made footprints on the freshly-cleaned tatamis and the "engawa" (boarded floor). They came like a storm and ravaged the whole house. My mother just didn't know how to stop it. The worst was the time when they found "omanju" (Japanese cakes) in the cupboard.

Once I came home with "omanju" I had just bought. One of the hungry boys was sitting there. I said to myself: "Oh, no." I knew my mother would not stand up for us. I so wanted her to say: "Thank you, Misao-chan. Why don't you just put it away? We have a visitor now." But she didn't. The boy's eyes glared. Before I knew it, every particle of "omanju" was swallowed up in his stomach instead of ours.

Prior to the end of World War II, it was customary for a policeman to go around from house to house with a registration book checking each household. This was to make sure that no undesirable characters like communists, Korean or Chinese dissidents or democrats would be hiding in the household. When a policeman came around to our house, of course he found out that our father was Korean. When he found out that a pretty Japanese woman was living by herself with young children while her Korean husband was away, he wanted to sit down at the front foyer of the house and spend time chatting. Japanese men had a haughty notion that my mother would prefer a Japanese man to her Korean husband no matter what kind of trash he was.

If the policeman sat down, my mother felt obliged to offer him a cushion and some tea. This was the usual custom. Not offering tea would be the utmost insult. After all, one would not like to upset a policeman, especially when one's husband was a Korean. The police could arrest him under any pretext. The guy was so dense that he took no notice of my mother's face that was downcast with an invisible message of "Please, go away. Please, go away", and her answers were lukewarm noddings of her head.

At first, my elder sister and I would stand a broom upside-down, which was supposed to be an effective method of repelling unwanted guests. But after a while, when it did not seem to produce the desired result, I would come out and sidle up to my mother, saying: "Mommy, rice is boiling. What shall we do next?" This was usually effective. My mother would say hurriedly: "Excuse me, I must go and look." After the guest departed, we would sigh a sigh of relief, saying: "At last! I thought he would never leave." But it had to be I who would appear. Maybe due to my Korean blood or to my lack of respect for stupid adults, my face seemed to be imposing even as a child.

We also knew a couple by the name of W. Mr. W. was one of my father's classmates at the college. He married his first cousin. The couple inherited some money from the husband's family and was better off than we were. However, they were the most tight-fisted people I have ever known. The wife had a lot of kimonos, all silk. One day, they came to visit us while my father was away. The wife had a silk kimono on. We went out to a Japanese noodle shop. My mother, as usual, extravagantly ordered "tempura soba" (noodles with prawn tempura) but the Ws ordered plain "soba". After the order came and each started slurping one's order, Mrs. W lifted her head from her own bowl of noodles. "What are you all eating?" she asked.

"Tempura soba."

"How much is it?" My mother told her the price.

"Oh, my," she said in astonishment. She gave up the idea of spending so much money on a mere bowl of noodles and decided to be content with her plain noodles.

When we left the noodle shop, the sky was grey. By the time we walked over to our house, drops of rain started falling. Mrs. W. was worried that her silk kimono would get wet and be ruined. Japanese silk is spoiled easily by water. "Why don't you change to my cheaper kimono and take yours in a "furoshiki" (a square piece of material used for wrapping things)?"

My mother had only two kimonos, one made of cheaper material and the other of good silk crepe. Mrs. W. immediately agreed. She took off her kimono and put on my mother's. The kimono, that looked so nice on my mother, looked awful on her. She folded hers, wrapped it in a furoshiki and carried it as if she had been carrying something precious.

The W. couple had no children. The husband, who was equally stingy, once went on a company excursion to a hot spring resort. Since he was tight fisted, he usually refrained from any kind of relationships with women. In those days, men went freely to brothels or otherwise bought women. He, I think, was envious of these men but dared not do it because it would cost him money. But on this excursion, the expenses were paid by the company and at a hot spring resort, there were plenty of women for entertainment. So he went with a woman and promptly contracted gonorrhea. This was why they had no children.

Around this time Japan was deeply involved in the war with China and a shortage of resources was becoming apparent. We started queuing up for foods like bread, cake, milk and other necessities. The shops sometimes opened their doors suddenly and sold the goods to whoever happened to be lucky enough to be passing by. One sunny day, the Ws and we went for a walk to the nearby stream. Since they had no children and had money enough, they did not have to work too hard and had a lot of time that they did not know how to kill. So they often came to see us. As we were walking, Mrs. W. called out to me, "How much is the hat you have on?"

"One Yen and twenty-five sen."

She gasped, "My, so expensive? Why do you have to wear a hat?" Inside, I despised her. My only deterrent to calling her a fool was the manners I learned towards grown-ups. I ran ahead and heard her words at my back: "Children need not to dress up."

Then we happened to be passing by a bakery shop that had just opened to sell some bread. They rationed the number of loaves according to the number of family members. My mother got two loaves because we were four, including my younger sister, Keiko.

The Ws got just one loaf. With the newly-purchased bread, we walked over to the bank of the stream and sat down on the grass of the bank to eat the bread. My mother opened the package and each of us started tearing a piece of bread from a loaf. The Ws did not open their package. Mrs. W. held it closely to her breast. Their eyes were on our bread. After a few minutes of their staring, my mother could not contain herself. She offered our bread to them. This was what they were waiting for. So they ate the bread that belonged to the children while they guarded their bread like a treasure. I am sorry that they had not enjoyed life by spending their money while they could. After the defeat of Japan, the government changed the currency and the Ws would have lost all their money anyway.

chapter VIII

With my sister going to a Christian school, a lot of Western influence came into our family. However, even before that, my father, who liked modern things, used to take us to foreign films—mainly American. He hated Japanese films in which the heroine walked up and down, back and forth, without speaking a line and without making any decisions. (This was the way women were supposed to behave in those days. Any woman, who had an opinion of her own, like me, was shunned.) He dragged us to Charlie Chaplin's films and this is why I saw "City Life", "Modern Times" and others at the tender age of ten or eleven. For the same reason, I saw French films of love stories and Deanna Durbin's debut film, "The Girl of Orchestra." My father also liked to eat Western-style foods, so he used to take us to Suehiro Steak House after a promenade in the streets of Ginza. "Ginbura" (promenade in Ginza) was a fashionable thing to do. It was a sort of moving salon of intellectuals, artists and the well-to-do, where people met their friends. After dinner at Suehiro, my father bought éclairs instead of "manju".

Once, we went to see a film at the Toyoko Movie Theatre, and after the film, we went to the Grill, which was located downstairs in the same building. To my horror, I discovered one of the servers was a former classmate of my sister's. She was one of the girls who went to a commercial school and the school sent her to this restaurant to do her practicum. Even as a child, I was always keenly aware of social discrepancies. Later when I grew up, I realized that social problems were not a matter of black and white and far more complex than I thought. But when I was a child, I was on the side of the poor. When I saw how humiliating it must be for this girl to serve the family of her classmate, the food stuck in my throat. The whole family fidgeted and left without enjoying the food.

Since Keisen had some American influences, they had good, well-educated and enlightened teachers, one of whom was a proper organ teacher. By then, our harmonium had been upgraded to a proper organ. So my sister started taking proper lessons, much to my envy and chagrin. A young lady teacher, who lived in a quiet middle-class suburb, taught the lessons. It was customary for young children, who were taking lessons, to carry a red briefcase in which they put their music sheets. The red briefcase was a symbol of taking music lessons. My mother did not buy my sister that coveted red briefcase. Due to the shortage of materials caused by the war with China (Japan meant to defeat China in two months but instead, the war dragged on into the third year), there were not any to buy.

The music teacher was a daughter of a family of reasonable means. When my sister went for a lesson on a warm summer day, her mother came out with a glass of lemonade. My sister practiced at first but soon slackened off. When she did not practice, my mother gave her a lecture.

After a while of her intense playing, we got an anonymous postcard. It said: "Please, don't play the organ constantly. I get a headache when I hear it." My mother, who was susceptible to any comment or gossip, got sick. Her nerves were shot. The fact that we did not know who sent it, made it worse. She became suspicious of every neighbour around us. When I came home from school one day, my mother was in bed. I can't remember where my younger sister was. She called out from her bed that she could not prepare a snack because she was sick, and that I should slice a piece of bread and make it myself. I took the loaf of bread out of the pantry and tried to cut a piece of it, but I was a spoiled child and had never cut bread before. All housekeeping chores were performed by my mother and my sister. The first thing I did was to cut my own finger instead of the bread. As red blood oozed out of my finger, my mother had to get out of bed and treat it.

Our neighbour on the south side of our house came to visit and comfort my mother. She was a widow and was also running a boarding house for the male students who were attending the nearby veterinarian school. Being of the age when their sexual curiosity ran rampant and with their knowledge of anatomy, they were bursting out in acne.

Mrs. Ono had a young daughter about the same age as my sister. The constant presence of young men in the same house was making her bloom prematurely into a young woman. Her skin was moist and her lips were red. She was conscious of the men. My mother warned us against these students. As our upstairs' windows faced the Ono's windows, we were told to shut the paper screen doors when we were upstairs.

Mrs. Ono was pre-maturely old because of her hard life, but she was a good-natured, kind woman. She had no prejudice towards my mother, who was a Korean's wife. She did not hesitate to come over at my mother's beckoning and spend hours listening to my mother.

The Onos had a female cat and one day she produced kittens. The oldest of the litter had a limp and was not very bright. But the next born was pretty and intelligent. Her fur was mainly white with black and orange patches. She and I hit it off immediately. She moved from next door to my bedroom. During the night, she would roam around and come home to me at around 2:00 a.m. She would sit at my head and meow. When I raised my covers, she would crawl in and share my pillows. Life went on happily for a while until one day, my mother found out, to her horror, that the cat, Mimi, was using the flower arrangement basins for her litter. In hindsight, she was clever because that's what a litter box looks like and she was not spoiling the tatamis. But we didn't know that. To make the matter worse, my lips started to get swollen. A doctor told my mother that I must be allergic to the cat's fur.

My mother gave the cat to the barber's family known to us. After a while, his wife brought the cat back. They could not manage the cat either. It cost money to keep a pet. When they came, I was sick in bed. But I got out of bed to see the cat. Mimi was sitting right outside of the door and meowed loudly at the sight of me. She had a collar, made of red crepe material, but she somehow looked shabby and rough. It struck me that the living conditions of an animal would have a strong influence on it. She pleaded loudly that she wanted to stay.

"Mummy, she is crying. She wants to stay here," I said to my mother. Her reply was half hearted. Her mind was made up not to keep her. Since I was not in the position to manage the family purse, I could not insist. I might not have been able to keep her later anyway. There was a great shortage of food for human beings and every pet had to be put down towards the end of the War. But at that moment, Mimi and I sat together in great sorrow.

And my heart broke.

We soon found out who had sent us the postcard telling us not to play the organ so much. It was the female dentist who lived across the street. In those days, a female dentist was a rare phenomenon. She was married to an ordinary salary man and had two daughters. The younger of them was about my age and was pretty. They found out that this daughter had tuberculous adenitis of the hilum. Mrs. Wada obviously took it as a punishment for her writing an anonymous letter to us. She asked my mother to come over so that she could confess and ask for forgiveness. I don't know why I accompanied my mother but I was there. Maybe my mother did not have the courage to face her alone. I saw this woman's face contorted with remorse and with tears that streamed down her cheeks. Her words came out of her mouth in fragments between her wailings and sobs. She held my mother's hands tightly and told her that she had been envious of our Sunday outings. She enviously watched my father take his family out; whereas her Japanese husband never took them out and they had a dull life. I realized for the first time that going out every Sunday was a special treat and there were people who could be envious of Koreans.

She loved her daughter, who was sick, and she would have done anything to save her life. I can't remember whether my mother spoke the words of forgiveness or not. But I forgave her. I was not that worried when I saw that postcard. Not knowing the culprit was annoying, but with the riddle solved, being half Korean, I didn't care. I felt sorry for the woman who was in such a mental state. My mother must have consoled her because we did get away at some point.

We saw her daughter everyday. My mother had taken care of me when I had the same illness and she sent me to a specialist who eventually cured me. But Mrs. Wada obviously did not know how to treat her sick daughter. We could see that the illness was advancing. She had a beautiful, almost transparent, complexion with rosy cheeks. But she kept on playing with other children everyday until it got dark and even in damp weather. We knew that she should have been inside the house but Mrs. Wada, despite her worries, left her outside. A little while later, we moved so we never found out what happened to that poor little girl.

chapter IX

*I*t finally became my turn to graduate from the elementary school and go to "joggakko". Towards the end of the school days at the public school, I was fed up with my classmates who had a different lifestyle. I wanted to get out of this uncouth environment as quickly as I could. I longed for another lifestyle that had a little more culture. Shortly before graduation (since I knew that I had been accepted by Keisen), I did not even want to go to school. Almost everyday I claimed a stomach ache that mysteriously cleared up by the afternoon. To enter Keisen, I did not even have to go through rigorous preparation for the entrance examination. The Ministry of Education changed the system and the selection of students was to be based solely on their transcripts. My luck followed me all through my life (or went ahead?) and I never had to take any entrance examinations.

The teacher, who taught the sixth grade, usually raised the marks slightly, but within reason, of those who were going to "joggakko". They started doing this some time before the last school year so that it would not look suspiciously abrupt. Consequently, my report card was almost straight "ko"s (A) with the exception of one "otsu" (B) in physical education. I suppose even Mr. Nasumoto could not do anything about it. I was so bad at it.

One day, Mr. Nasumoto called pupils one by one into the classroom to tell them about their transcripts. Since Mr. Ono started visiting us, Mr. Nasumoto distanced himself from us and the relationship between us was rather cool. So I was a bit wary about what he might have written in my transcript. He took my transcript in his hands and read out in a level voice: "This pupil is highly intelligent. She is a great reader and has read extensively. She is also very responsible and has held the position of vice-president for two terms. Her performance is excellent. "

"Is this satisfactory to you?" Mr. Nasumoto smiled at me kindly after he had finished reading. I was impressed by his male objectivity and the impartial, rational attitude of a university graduate. I nodded, pleased.

Now, the only thing remaining was the interview at the "joggakko". The day of the interview was a grey rainy day in between winter and spring. I knew the school took students mostly based on connection, but my heart still pounded a bit. Miss Miyazaki, the interviewer, was a Christian-looking single lady with grey hair. I sat rigidly in front of her. "What is the reason you chose this school?"

"Because my sister…" I didn't even get to finish the sentence.

"Very good. Now you may go." That was it. After a few days of anxious waiting, I got a letter from the school telling me that I was accepted.

In the meantime, in 1938, the Japanese government passed a law forcing every Korean to change their names into Japanese. Maybe they wanted to recruit young Korean men for more manpower for the war and the Korean names stood in the way. Whatever the reason, it did ease up the situation for people like us. My sisters and I did not look Korean to Japanese eyes (we did, actually) and we had no accent. So, on the surface, we stopped getting that peculiar look of wonder when people heard our Korean name. On the other hand, it complicated the situation in a different way. Now we had to disclose verbally the fact that we were half Korean. The question became "when?", "how?" and "should we tell them?" "Would they change their attitude if they found out?"

The war was getting worse. Japan was stuck in the mud from which they simply did not know how to extricate themselves. At every household where there was a healthy young man, we could see banners standing, indicating that he was called to the war. The family that was left behind without a bread earner had to struggle to survive. There was nobody else to replace him. Every time when I saw the banners, I felt a cold shiver, thinking: "What would happen to us if my father got drafted?" Very fortunately, they didn't want old Koreans in their sacred war.

The Japanese military's propaganda made me sick. They called the war sacred and sang praises of the brotherhood of Asian countries (Japan, Korea, China and Manchuria; of course, Japan would be the leader). I wanted to know how they were going to establish a unified Asia when they could not even accept Korea as an equal. I despised their fake slogans.

Actually, intelligent Japanese men were trembling that the axe of conscription might fall upon their heads. The Japanese army's sergeants and corporals came mainly from the working classes and were notorious for their unreasonably mean treatment of the soldiers in the lower ranks. They made the army life a hell on earth. (It was amusing to see them suddenly turn into meek pacifists the minute Japan surrendered.) There was a physical examination to determine whether one was fitted or not to serve in the army. So if one got drafted, there were several methods to make oneself sick on the day of the physical examination. One recommended method was to drink one litre of soy sauce. It caused one to look pale and haggard. Some simply fasted for days and grew a beard, which made them look shabby and sick.

At the corners of busy streets, women were asking the passers-by to make a knot in a long piece of cotton with red lines on it. This was called "senninbari" (one thousand stitches). After one thousand women had made a knot in the red thread, it was sent to a soldier who would wrap it around his waist so that he would be protected from harm and remain safe. In fact, this piece of material proved to be rather unsafe, or rather unhealthy. In war conditions, when soldiers had to lie on the ground and not take baths for days, this became a wonderful nest for fleas, ticks and Nanking bugs.

The people in Japan had no inkling of what was going on at the front and why their country was slowly marching into destruction. Things were getting scarcer day by day. Many items were now rationed. Rice, tobacco, sugar, sake and fabrics, such as silk and cotton, disappeared from the shops. The only fabric we could get was some shiny, cheap-looking synthetics. If there had been fabrics, there were no notions with which to sew them. We had to take old garments apart, pulling out the thread carefully, so that we could use it again on the new fabric.

The government decreed useless, rigid rules, as if these rules were going to help the country win the war. One of the rules was that all schools had to have uniforms. Keisen previously had no uniform, but now we had to wear blue serge pleated skirts and blue serge sailor tops in winter, and the same skirt and a white sailor top in summer. In both seasons, we wore a tie on the front of the blouse. The colour of the tie and the number of braids on the collar of the top were different according to each school.

There was a special art to pressing this pleated skirt. Since Japanese bedding is laid on tatami mats, we peeled up the lower "futon" (mattress), placed our skirt, carefully straightening the pleats, and laid the "futon" back on the top of it. Thus the skirt would be pressed while we slept on it. Sometimes the skirt got the lines of the tatami mats on it. In order to avoid this happening, we placed a piece of newspaper under the skirt and put the "futon" back.

So when I finally got to Keisen, we didn't have those pretty little things my sister had. It therefore, lost some lustre.

There was one thing I loved to do and to which I was looking forward. That was to take the commuter trains. Anybody who took the commuting trains regularly would buy a season pass to save some money. One put this pass in a celluloid holder (there was no plastic then) and showed it to the employees of the railroad, who stood in a small wooden wicket watching. Students often hung it around their necks by a string or put it in a breast pocket to facilitate taking it out to show it. We were warned by our parents not to show the name and the address written on the pass to anybody, so that we would not be harassed. Equally, we were advised never to drop it, so that it would not fall into the wrong hands.

I was so delighted to show this pass. It made me feel so grown up. The day before I was to start school, I practised the art of showing the pass at home. My mother thought I was too childish. She could not appreciate that I, with a peculiar artistic temperament, stayed childlike even when I got older chronologically. She was normal. The world expected everyone to act according to the so-called normal standard and I was out of it. Since we had to take three different lines to get to Keisen, I would have a lot of opportunities to show the pass.

At Keisen, unlike the elementary school, they did not call classes by numbers. Each class had the name of a flower. For instance, the classes were called: Cherry, Plum, Mum, Pine and others. In order to let students befriend everyone and to prevent them from forming certain groups, the school shuffled the students each year and regrouped them. There were only two classes in each year. When I entered the school, they had to enlarge the classes slightly, but my sister's class had only a little over thirty students. My class must have had between forty and fifty students.

Since the school was established on Christian principles, there was absolutely no racial discrimination. There were Chinese, Taiwanese and Korean students. There were also quite a few "Nisei" (second generation Japanese born in North America) girls who had come to study Japanese and got stuck in Japan at the outbreak of the War. They were older than the rest of the class and their Japanese was imperfect, but nobody cared. Towards the end of World War II, our class had one girl, who was a mixture of German and Japanese parents, and two Turkish girls. After the War, the German girl climbed up onto the roof of their house (I don't know why she was doing this) and fell to the ground. She seemed to be all right, so she got up and laughed at herself. Then she had dinner and went to bed. She passed away during the night.

The Turkish girls knew Japanese well enough to follow the school curriculum. There had always been a large colony of Turks in Japan. In the area quite close to the school (about two railway stations away), there was a Turkish mosque and quite a few Turks lived in the vicinity. They all spoke fluent Japanese. Since the activities of foreigners were regarded with suspicion by the military government, those two girls must have been forced to come to the Japanese school. The government had closed all the foreign schools.

On the first day at Keisen, each girl was assigned a student from the upper classes so that the helper could break the new girl into school life. The girls were gentler than the ones I knew at the elementary school because they came from a better class. The teachers were Christians and the toilet was clean.

But the most impressive thing for me was the teaching about God. Since I was sickly from the age of seven, I used to wonder what would happen to me when I died. I was afraid of death. I always wanted to know what would happen when my life on earth was terminated. There were several philosophical questions that troubled my little head. Why does yesterday never come back? In Tokyo, in those days, the road conditions were not very good. After a rainy day, a lot of potholes in the road were filled with dirty water. On the water, the residue of the oil from automobiles shimmered in rainbow colours. Once, I passed by one of them, stopped and looked at the iridescent colours. I went a few yards ahead and then returned to the puddle. "But this is not the moment I was here before. A few minutes have passed. Why can't I go back exactly to the same moment I was here before? Why does the earth go only ahead and never backwards?" It drove me crazy thinking about it.

Also I wanted to know which came first, an egg or a hen. A hen, an egg, a hen, an egg. What is the beginning? Where did it start? Actually, this question had been solved before I went to this school. My elder sister was hiding her textbooks in the closet upstairs. She had a peculiar sense of possessiveness and used to hide her textbooks from me because I would read them even before she opened the first page.

She was not particularly spiritually inquisitive and slow to be touched by spiritual teachings.

So we did not know that she was taking Bible study classes at school. On this particular day, I was sick and absent from school, but my sister was at school. So I opened the closet and went through her textbooks. I came across the textbook on Bible study. It seemed easy to read. I opened the first page and read. I trembled with a mysterious feeling of joy and revelation for it said: "God is the being who made everything and keeps them. He is everywhere." It was as if a grey cloud lifted from my consciousness. Everything was solved instantly. At the same time I became afraid that this Almighty Being might see how bad I was. After this experience, I was no longer so afraid of dying. I knew it was not all dark on the other side.

A day at Keisen began with worship, a spiritual talk by one of the teachers, prayer and hymn singing. I loved the talks given by the teachers. Some were better than others. The best speaker was, however, the headmistress, Michi Kawai. I have, in my past life, seldom heard such a wonderful speaker as she. She was concise, clear with her ideas, and interesting. Her talks invariably ended within twenty minutes, no less, no more. We could watch the clock and see that every single one of her talks finished exactly in twenty minutes. That was all the time she needed to get her message across.

The worst speaker was Mr. Tanaka. There were not many male teachers in this all girls' school but there were about four male teachers. One taught horticulture, one chemistry, one art and one science. The one who taught science was Mr. Tanaka. He was such a nice, good-natured person. Consequently, he couldn't be crisp and curt. One morning, he went on and on. I guessed that he didn't know himself how to put an end to his talk. Miss Kawai, who like any other intelligent person, did not have much patience or tolerance for slow and stupid people. At first she looked at her watch, then got up from her chair (the day's speaker and the headmistress sat on a platform, so we could see what she was doing) and started pacing up and down irritated. Mr. Tanaka took the hint and hurriedly said: "That is all," and made a short quick bow like a piston.

The story told by Miss Miyazaki especially impressed me. It was about a woman who was poor and used to peddle oranges. She made efforts to better herself and her life improved. She rose to a high position. On the evening of a celebration, a woman came up to her and said: "Didn't you use to peddle oranges, calling out: "'Mikan', 'mikan' (orange, orange,)?"

The lady smiled and said: "Oh, no, if you call out the way you did, you would never be able to sell any oranges. I will demonstrate it for you. Listen," and she called out in a clear voice: "M-e-e-kan, M-e-e-kan."

We sang a lot of hymns. I loved music and singing hymns gave me great joy. If there was any kind of crisis, we had a prayer meeting. Whenever there was any occasion that someone needed help, we had a gathering and prayed. I learned to pray and I started praying before I went to bed.

Believing in God made me an optimistic person. Although my faith was not yet so firm and I still had a lot to learn, now I had a norm to follow. Most of the teachers were unmarried, but they were content, happy and resigned. They did not get hysterical like other old maids. They knew that each person had a different vocation and a single life was their God-given vocation. The teachers in art and music were professionals. The art teacher was a dandy young fellow who had studied in Paris. He brought to class the air of Paris by wearing a bow tie. I never thought myself good at art but he saw my artistic (peculiar) temperament. One day I was surprised to discover that my drawing was displayed on the wall of the hallway. He continually displayed my works after that.

The school was not upper class like the Convent of the Sacred Heart, which I later attended. But it had many students with unique interesting backgrounds. A girl in my class was a granddaughter of a very famous writer and a daughter of a very famous painter. She played the piano beautifully and had a good sense of pitch. She later studied Russian and became a writer of children's literature.

There was also a daughter of a well-known translator of foreign books. In those days, her father and another man were doing almost all of the translation of foreign books. Her name was Nana, taken from Emile Zola's famous novel.

There was a niece of a famous evangelist, Toyohiko Kagawa. Rev. Kagawa was a famous preacher and was doing a lot of charitable works in a poor section of Tokyo. His own daughter was in my sister's class and his niece was in my class. Once, I visited their house and came out determined that I would never marry a pastor or a Christian who sacrificed himself for the good of others. I did not see any merit in giving up one's life to such an extent that one always lived in an uncomfortable house, short of money and consequently losing one's looks. I always believed in keeping one's looks and living a reasonably comfortable life. I would not have bought two fur coats when others were starving nor would I have spent hours smearing on lipstick or be totally uncompassionate, but I did not think that it was right to look miserable and poor just because one was a Christian. Surely, God must love beautiful things? To me, it was not wrong "to love oneself as thy neighbour." If one were to love one's neighbour as one's self, one must love one's self first. If I were to lead a life totally dedicated to others, I would become a nun or remain single. But it's all up to the vocation God gives me.

In one of my other classes, there was a niece of a very famous xylophone player and he came to our school to give a concert. Another time, my sister and I got to go to a concert given by a famous teenaged violinist, Toshiya Eto, who was accompanied by his sister, Reiko. The Eto family had some connection with our school. They both went to study at the University of Arts' music department where my sister later studied, too. Toshiya was the first Japanese musician to go to Julliard after World War II.

The school had adopted a blind Chinese girl and sponsored her education. Once, she came to visit the school. The school also invited one of the Japanese missionaries, working in China, to give a lecture on the cultural differences between China and Japan.

Our minds were broadened by various ways. We had a lot of second-generation Japanese Americans and Canadians who had come to study Japanese at our school. Since their knowledge of Japanese was not so advanced, some of them were in lower grades than the classes where they should have been. But nobody took notice of it. Some girls who came from the countryside were sometimes put back a year. Nobody cared how much older they were than we. In hindsight, I think those girls had a certain advantage over us because one year makes a lot of difference in maturity and they had more skill in handling certain things.

Two-thirds of my class were taking music lessons and the rest were studying Japanese ballet, Western ballet, koto (a Japanese string musical instrument) and other forms of art. Actually 90% of the class could afford some extra-curricular lessons.

I soon became noted for reading difficult books with tremendous speed. I got to know a girl by the name of Keiko Tsubaki. She had a brother who was going to university. Keiko soon became a victim to my avid reading.

"Ask your brother to lend me such and such a book." Then it went as follows:

"Brother, please let me lend that book to Miss Morimoto."

"I never lend books."

"Oh, but she keeps the books so neatly, and she is very reliable. She will definitely return the book in beautiful condition."

"She won't understand the book. It's too mature for a girl of your age."

"Oh, but she understands it. She is very mature. She reads all adult books. Pl-e-a-s-e."

"Oh, well, you may take it, then."

The next day, she came to school, smiling. "My brother finally said 'yes'." Thus, I got to read Emile Zola's "Nana", Auguste Strindberg's "Idiot", "Gentlemen Prefer Blondes" and many others.

I was also noted in the class as the fastest reader who kept the borrowed books clean. If I found a book lying on someone's desk, I would flip through it and would say: "Whose book is this? May I borrow it?" Someone would call out to the owner of the book: "Someone wants to borrow your book."

"Who is it?"

"Morimoto-san."

"Of course. If it's Morimoto-san, she may borrow it. She keeps the book clean and she reads so fast."

Because of the vast amount of reading, I could read almost every Chinese character I came across. One day Noguchi-san said to me: "Nobody, but nobody, has ever read my mother's name correctly so far."

"Urn. How do you write it?" She showed me a complicated Chinese character that made up the word "embroidery", together with another Chinese character. After glancing at it once, I announced, "Nuiko". Her mouth opened in astonishment. After a few seconds of silence, she said: "You are the first person who has ever read it correctly."

Books were my world. I didn't want to do anything else as long as I was reading. I even wanted to read during mealtimes. Unfortunately, soon my interest had to be focused on food rather than reading, because Japan declared war on the U.S.A. by attacking Pearl Harbour and food disappeared almost completely from Tokyo.

chapter X

Our most unique teacher was Mrs. Chigira, a stern teacher of history and geography. She always wore a traditional Japanese kimono and had her hair pulled back in a chignon. The rumour was that she was the wife of a physician who worked at the Ministry of the Imperial Household. Her skin was rather brown, an unwelcome colour in Japan, where fair skin is regarded as more beautiful. She was remote from the concept of womanliness. She looked as though she skipped the usual process of going from a shy young bride to a young mother to a plump chatty middle-aged housewife to the final stage of a mean mother-in-law, but ended up at the final stage of a strict mother-in-law in a flash. She was strict but not mean. She was also fair. But she could not tolerate stupidity.

In class, if she named someone to answer a question, she would wait only one second. If no answer came after one second, her sharp impatient voice would ring in the classroom: "Next." Thus, while the girls sat in stony silence and shame, her voice would command: "Next", "Next", and "Next". However, whenever it became my turn, I always knew the correct answer. The girls would sigh with relief because her question would stop at my place with her "yoroshii" (very good). One day, one of the girls exclaimed: "Oh, good! You are here today. I was afraid you might be absent. Today, we have Mrs. Chigira's class."

Once, after a class project, she named three girls' works for distinction. Not only was I included in the three, but she also said it was the best work in the whole class.

Mrs. Chigira harboured a lot of social indignation. Whenever there was a topic she wanted to discuss, she would stop teaching and start to talk about that subject. Whenever she said, "Everyone," we would grin and shut our textbooks because she would go on discussing the subject till the end of the class. We all loved her "osekkyo" (sermons). She gave us lectures on "Why We Should Be Charitable", "What Goes Out Comes Around", "How a Wife Should Behave Towards Her Mother-in-law" and others.

I always think that Keisen taught two subjects especially well. One was English. We had English classes almost everyday and for conversation classes, a native speaker (mostly American-Japanese) was assigned as a teacher. The other subject was music.

The school hired professional musicians who were actually performers. A lot of girls could play the piano and the whole school was musical. The music teacher, Miss Saito, was in her thirties and had come back from the U.S.A., where she had been studying voice. She was an artist and, with the mannerisms she acquired in the U.S.A., she was a bit out of the ordinary. But she introduced us to foreign music which the majority of the Japanese did not know. Her examinations were quite different and professional. We had to sight read and sing one of the tunes in the book. I remember once one of them was Chopin's so-called lullaby. Since I was not taking piano lessons (I taught myself how to read music and play the organ), I was not very good at sight-reading. So I got Lisa Uchida to sing them for me and I memorized the tunes. Miss Saito always dismissed me with "Very good", at the end of my singing.

Miss Saito stayed single until after the War. She was over forty when she got married. While she was working as a singer, she had a male agent, who was about seven years younger than she was. He was not married and lived with his parents. One day his mother declared that she was quitting the job of looking after him.

"I am getting old and tired. Go and find a woman who will cook and do laundry for you. Hurry up."

He said he was not going to look. If he had to marry, he would marry Miss Saito. So they got married. He was a tall, rather handsome fellow. Even after they got married, they kept the lifestyle they had before their marriage. Off she would go away to the U.S.A. for work and leave her husband alone in Japan. But they were happy.

Mr. Aketagawa was our art teacher. As I mentioned before, he studied in Paris and brought back the artistic atmosphere of French culture. In those days people travelled by ship and the trip was expensive. So they did not travel so frequently. Anybody who had been to the Western world, where white people lived, was regarded with awe. Mr. Aketagawa had a medium build, had thick curly hair and wore glasses.

Being an artist, he probably could see and liked my artistic temperament, which was merely peculiar to others. In one art class, I wanted to keep on reading "Nana" by Emile Zola, instead of paying attention to the drawing. I secretly placed the book on my lap and kept on reading, while I pretended to draw. A couple of meanies in the next room, who were peeping through the little holes in the partition wall, saw what I was doing. They shouted out loud: "Morimoto-san is not drawing! Bad girl! She is reading a book instead!" I raised my face and my eyes met with those of Mr. Aketagawa. He averted his eyes. He obviously said to himself: "Women!" But he could not ignore them either. So he pretended to look at each student's work. He started walking down the aisle slowly, turning his head right and left. I was always at the very back of the classroom because I was the tallest girl in class. He took a long time, giving me ample time to hide the book. By the time he reached me, "Nana" was safely tucked away inside the desk. He might have approved of me even more if he found out that I was reading that naughty French book.

Miss Takano was a sewing teacher and I remember her even unto this day as one of the people who influenced me deeply. At the time, I was too young to truly appreciate her. All I knew was that she was an extremely nice person, but as the years passed by and I matured, I came to appreciate her more and more and I think she was one of the purest human beings I have ever met.

She had a face like what the Japanese would call "a Pekinese sneezing." All her facial features seemed to come together in the center of her face. Her skin was rather brown. She always wore a traditional Japanese kimono. Although she was not beautiful, she was always smiling and had a heart of gold. When my elder sister, who was good with her hands, presented her beautifully-sewn home assignment of "yukata" (an unlined cotton kimono), she was surprised. She obviously thought that since our father was Korean, we would not know how to make a kimono. But this misconception worked fine with me. She did not know that my inability to sew was due to my incapability and not to my being half Korean. So when I could not sew anything, she treated me with leniency.

Because of the War, it was getting increasingly difficult to get material and notions, so we were told to undo an already made-up kimono and bring it. While we were undoing the kimono, we were to save the thread and use it again. This is one main reason why I never learned to make kimonos during my school years. My mother's kimonos were all cut and sewn in a professional manner due to her training. She did not want me to disturb anything because what we were learning was school sewing. I might have learned a little more, if I could get a piece of brand new material which I was allowed to cut and sew according to the teacher's instructions. But as I was forbidden to cut and sew, I just sat there, holding my mother's kimono. Consequently, I understood nothing about the pattern and the folding of a scaled-down sample.

As I proved to be absolutely incompetent and useless in sewing, Miss Takano called me one day to have a word. "Next semester, your class is going to make a lined adult kimono but you may make a baby's vest. When you go home, tell your mother that and get the material for a 'chanchanko' (a vest)." This became a family joke but I can't remember whether or not I was able to even finish that.

Any teacher, who had a small heart, would have given me an F or at least a C for my sewing but she didn't. She kept on giving me a B. As I had nothing to do during the two-hour sewing class, I sat next to Yoko, who was an excellent sewer, and held a sleeve of the kimono she was sewing, and literally jabbered about nonsense. When my voice got louder and too annoying, Miss Takano would call out, "Girls, girls, stop talking and do some work, please." She would have fainted if she had found out that I later went to a dress designing school and can now sew beautifully. I owe it to her. How grateful I am!

We also had another famous professional musician, Mr. Koten Okuda. He was supposed to be the best organist in the whole of Japan. But due to politics among the professors (it was rumoured that Mr. Okuda trod upon some important toe), he could not get a professorship at the Tokyo Conservatory of Music (later the University of Arts). I learned early that becoming a university professor was not totally about merit, but politics played an important role. Like Mozart, who was extremely talented but died in poverty because he lost the protection of the Archbishop of Salzburg, a lot of talents are not appreciated and ignored due to insidious politics.

So Mr. Okuda had a position at the famous Protestant school, Aoyama Gakuin. He not only taught music at our school but he was now my sister's organ teacher. The young lady, who had been teaching her, got married and stopped teaching. My mother took my sister to Mr. Okuda's house for her first lesson.

"How much do you charge for 'sokushu' (the initiation fee)?" she asked him.

"What is 'sokushu'?" was his reply.

Apparently, being an artist, he was not so concerned with worldly monetary matters. Later, my mother repeated continually, "He didn't even know what 'sokushu' was."

My mother asked him another question. "Do you ever get complaints about your playing?"

"Yes, I do," was the nonchalant reply.

"What do you do, then?"

"Nothing."

My mother was worried that since Mr. Okuda was so artistic that he might be temperamental. She instructed my sister that she should never cry in front of the teacher, if he ever scolded her harshly. "It's because he loves you and wants to teach you properly. If you cry even once, he will never scold you again and you will never be able to learn. You must only cry when you leave."

Mr. Okuda's wife was a graduate of the Tsuda English College. At the time of my mother's visit, they had just had their first baby. The baby's pram was standing in the foyer of the entrance with an English children's book casually placed in it. This scene appealed to my mother greatly. It had an air of modernism.

Mr. Okuda was later drafted and sent to Indonesia. After the War, he returned safely but only physically intact. He was so scarred spiritually, he forgot to smile anymore. His innocent trusting artist's soul was shattered by witnessing the atrocities the Japanese military inflicted on prisoners of war and the natives of Indonesia: he could not recover from the blow.

While he was still in Indonesia, he risked his life to let a famous American pianist, who was in the internment camp, give a secret concert. He apparently dared to light the hall with candles and let the foreign prisoners attend the concert. He obviously did as much as he could to help the foreign prisoners cope with their daily activities.

There was another Japanese captain who was kind to the foreigners in the internment camps in Indonesia. His name was Captain Tanaka. When I was studying at the Convent of the Sacred Heart, one of my schoolmates, Tina Muller, was a Dutch ambassador's daughter. She was in the internment camp as a baby. As the family had great difficulties getting milk for the baby, Captain Tanaka sneaked in milk for them and tried to ease the difficulties the family was experiencing. Later, this diplomat was stationed in Japan as an ambassador, and the family looked for Captain Tanaka. There was a happy reunion.

Even the Japanese army was not totally without men who had a heart.

chapter XI

It was becoming more and more apparent that my mixed blood isolated me from the world of the Japanese. I could never have chums as the other girls did. I was like a drop of oil on the surface of water. It never mingled but only floated. I was also quite masculine in a sense and that did not help. I was quite happy to do things by myself, whereas other girls were constantly grouping themselves. It seemed as if they always needed someone to prop themselves up. They seemed even unable to walk to the station alone. Sometimes a classmate would ask me to wait after school so that we could walk to the station together. So I had to wait around and it was very annoying. Later I discovered that this was a woman's innate nature which I lacked and hence, I was not very feminine.

Although I did not have a bosom friend, I did have some friends. I did get invited out by some of them and I did reciprocate. Our friendship was such that we never exchanged spiritual experiences and I never felt an urge to confide in them.

My future plans were also quite different from others. Whereas the ultimate purpose for other girls was to get married, I was not so keen about getting married and settling down. Also, I did not feel attracted to Japanese men. My blood rebelled against them.

Around this time, in my class, there was a girl by the name of Yoko. She was about two years older than we were and it made her a little more mature. She was a nice girl, full of fun.

She was intellectually not so brilliant but was good at many practical subjects that required common sense.

The family she was brought up in and living with, was not her own family. Her own blood family lived in Hokkaido, the northern part of Japan. When she was a little girl, the Higaki family happened to be visiting the area and fell in love with this little girl. With the permission of the family, they brought her back to Tokyo and were bringing her up as their own daughter. I think the parents, especially the mother, wanted to marry Yoko to one of their three sons.

The father owned a publishing company and the family was wealthy. Yoko was taking lessons in Japanese ballet, which was enormously expensive. She was already excellent in the art and was often on the stage with famous professional performers. She once happened to be on the same programme as a famous opera singer, Tamaki Miura.

Miss Miura was a great artist and like any other great artists often are, she was strange according to normal standards. She was a walking bundle of narcissistic self-confidence. She painted her face with thick rouge and other cosmetics and behaved childishly (not childlike). Yoko told me afterwards: "She squealed out in a childish voice 'my next number is — — —' and I was so embarrassed my cheeks went red (if one could see it through the thick stage make-up she had on for Japanese ballet) " and she imitated her voice.

Miss Miura was a true artist, who would disregard the so-called social customs, and dressed and talked the way she liked. That meant she was clad in a bright red kimono, something an ordinary Japanese married woman would never dare to wear. (Actually she was once married to an army officer but was later divorced.) This was in Japan prior to 1945. During World War II, she had no place in society and consequently died in poverty. In those days, the Western opera was not well known in Japan nor was any other type of classical Western music. So there was no place for her to earn a decent living.

During one sewing class, as I was sitting next to Yoko, yapping as usual, she said to me: "You are going to a higher educational institution, aren't you?"

"Yes, of course." I didn't understand why anyone wanted to stop studying after five years of lycée.

"I am not. I don't like school. So I am going to get married and have a nice family."

I thought that would be a good idea for her, too. Then she went on to tell me how cute her niece and nephew were, the kind of sentiment I failed to understand. She managed to be the second from the bottom of the class, which was a difficult achievement because one more slip and she would have failed. She later married a son of a very famous dress designer and became the good wife and mother she wanted to be.

Once, another classmate and I took her to a French film. There was one theatre in Tokyo that showed nothing but foreign films, mainly European films. (Since the beginning of the War, there were no more American films.) Mrs. Kawakita, who contributed so much by introducing foreign films to Japan, imported almost every single available German and French film. Towards the end of the War, she desperately looked for importable foreign films and we got to see even Argentine films.

As all Asian faces look alike to Westerners, all Westerners look the same to Asians. A lot of the Japanese would shun foreign films because they could not relate to the lifestyle and also could not distinguish one face from another. Yoko certainly belonged to the group that couldn't. The film we were watching was a part of "Les Misérables" with Danielle Darieux. After seeing two blond faces, she could not tell which one was which. She also did not even know this famous story. To make it worse, the film was long so it was in parts. She asked in a loud voice to our embarrassment: "What's she doing?", "Who is that one?"

We tried to whisper the answers in the beginning but it became too frequent. "Sh...h...h...h...," I said. "Shut up and just watch it." When we came out of the theatre, we were tired—she, from making efforts to comprehend and we, from trying to save ourselves from embarrassment and also trying to teach the basics of a foreign film to an ignorant movie goer.

As we got older, we naturally started getting curious about the secret life of a man and a woman. Bits and pieces of information started flying around. Knowledge-wise, I probably was the most profound scholar because of my reading, which included Auguste Strindberg's "Idiot". But

Yoko had an interest in this matter in a sweet humorous way. Her family structure was different from mine. She had brothers living under the same roof and since her father had money and position, her house had frequent guests, quite a few of whom were male: young army officers, publishers and company employees.

One day, she and I were sitting together on a commuter train going to school. She started snickering softly. So I asked: "What's wrong?" She whispered to me giggling:

"How can these grown-ups sit there, with sombre faces like that, after what they were doing last night?"

At school she told us: "Oh, my brother is so stupid", she giggled a few moments.

"Last night, we were sitting around in the "kotatsu" and my mother came in and said to my elder sister, '_____ —chan, you take a bath now' and my sister said, 'No, I can't, Mom. I have a visitor.'"

"My brother, who had been paying no attention to what we were doing, suddenly lifted his head and asked: 'Who is coming?' We cast our eyes downwards and were trying hard not to laugh but my brother kept on asking: 'Who is coming? Who is coming?' Oh, it was so funny."

Two years after graduation, Yoko fell in love with the son of a famous dress designer. Her foster mother, whose intention was to marry her to her own son, was upset and angry but the son himself gave her his sanction with the words: "You do what you think will make you happy." She became a good wife and mother.

chapter XII

*W*e moved again.

As Japan got stuck in the mud of the war against China (Japan did not call it a war. They called it an Incident) and the relationship with the U.S.A. was worsening, Japan was blockaded by the allied countries. Almost all forms of food disappeared from the city. Everything was rationed, from rice down to paper. Sometimes we had the ration tickets but there were no resources to back them up. The government allotted worthless government bonds to each family. Our family had to buy 50 yen worth bonds (a lot of money in those days) which, everyone knew, had absolutely no value. Women were told to give up their gold ornaments and thus my mother's rings disappeared. We saved silver wrappings of chocolates, rolled them into a ball and donated it to the government. Other families were surviving on the foods sent from relatives who lived in the countryside, but we did not have any relatives who could help us, so we had to depend entirely on the mercy of the merchants who were willing to sell goods at black market prices. Eventually, we couldn't do that either because there was simply nothing in the shops.

My mother heard the rumour that Kyodo, the area in which our school was located, had a little more food than the city because it was a suburb. So we decided to move there. When the landlord got our notice, he offered to cut the rent in half. He said that nobody, but nobody, kept the house so clean. We were the best tenants he had ever had.

But before we moved and while we were still in this house, permanent waves were imported, from a potential enemy country. The machine, that made the waves, was like an enlarged helmet or an upside-down "okama" (a rice cooker) from which numerous wires extended with pegs at the ends. It resembled an octopus clutching a woman's hair. The solution was strong and it stunk for hours afterwards. The whole process took many hours. The invention of permanent waves belonged to the country the Japanese government was trying to depict as an enemy, but women's desire to be beautiful superceded the cause.

My mother decided to get a perm. Maybe it was a joint decision between my father and mother because my father was babysitting for us children while my mother went to try this new invention. She left in the morning. I can't remember what we ate for lunch. It was a long time waiting. We waited, waited and waited. Now, none of the members who were waiting particularly excelled in housekeeping. If my father had turned on the gas and boiled water, we would have been lucky. So we just waited. In late afternoon, she finally came home. Our curious expectant gaze focused on her head. Since the invention was new and the technique still primitive, they could not adjust the strength of the curls. So the curls looked rather tight and did not suit her face. I remember we were all rather disappointed.

Moving to a new place was a complicated procedure. My mother had to do a lot of negotiating to hire a truck and get two men. Since there was a shortage of gasoline, one had to go a long way to get a truck that ran. To get two able-bodied men was an even more difficult task. Most young men were drafted and the men left were either middle-aged or old and they were suffering from malnutrition. But my mother managed to find two able-bodied men who had enough strength to carry heavy things. My mother, in those days, had to do a lot of negotiating using the skill she learned as a merchant's daughter and her charming good looks.

On the day of the move, there were cartons the men could not lift. My mother made a mistake of packing all the books in one carton and it weighed tons. I learned a lesson from this and later I was always careful to mix books with other items so that the movers could lift the boxes. I don't know how they managed it but we arrived at the new house in Kyodo.

It was one of three newly built houses. The house on the right side of ours, the end house on the block, was an older house. This older house belonged to an older couple by the name of No. Mr. No, who hovered around in the house in a kimono, was once a very wealthy man who worked in the financial world. He lost his fortune overnight by investing in bad stocks. They had to give up their beautiful house, sell everything and move to this tiny house in Kyodo, a countryside compared with the area in the city where they used to live. When they had to give up their grand piano, one of the daughters took a rag and polished it carefully, saying: "Go to the people who will love you."

Mrs. No, although she was no longer young, had a beautiful classical Japanese face. She was trying to earn a living by sewing kimonos for clients. This was a drastic descent for her into a lower class and her pride was constantly hurt. One of the daughters had already been married but this sudden disgraceful fall of her "jikka" (the family one originally comes from) hurt her position in her husband's family. She came to visit her parents in secret. She came quietly and left quietly.

The youngest daughter lived with her parents and was working. She was hit the hardest by her father's downfall. Now passed marriageable age, with parents with no social standing, all young men in the war and her being a working girl, she almost had no prospect of marriage. She quietly went in and out of the house with a resigned air. Mr. No must have been the happiest person in the family. He was suffering from dementia caused by the shock of losing his fortune overnight. He did not care that his wife had to make kimonos until her finger tips became sore or that Japan was entangled in the war and things were rationed. He was still living the peaceful life he was accustomed to. In the afternoon he would say in a nonchalant voice: "Shall we have tea now?" It drove Mrs. No up the wall.

On the other side of us, another of the three new houses was occupied by a couple about the same age as my parents. I can't remember any children so I guess they had none. As my father was absent from home, working in China, Mr. Majima was away from home almost all the time. But there was a big difference between the two men. My father may have been away from home but he would have been gladly with us if he could. He loved his family and missed it. But Mr. Majima rather enjoyed being away from his wife and did not come home very often. He was supposedly working for the independence of India. In those days, there were many Japanese who were supposedly working for an Asian cause, but in fact, they were often spending time with women, drinking and talking about causes with empty words.

The third new house at the corner belonged to a high-ranked banker. He was also away in Hong Kong. His wife, who looked like an ex-geisha, kept to herself. She had her hair coiled up on the top of the head (we called it up-style) and wore a fashionable short "haori" (top coat). Once, when there was an exercise for an air raid, we were standing around doing nothing, because these exercises were perfunctory and meaningless. We just had to obey the government's order even if it was stupid. Since we were idle, the women were talking.

Mrs. Kojima turned to Mrs. No and said: "Isn't this a waste of time? You could have sewn a kimono in the meantime." I don't think she meant ill because it was a fact. But Mrs. No's pride was stung and she was livid.

After World War II started and Japanese armies invaded Hong Kong, Mrs. Majima's husband's safety was in jeopardy. But the evening edition of Asahi Newspaper, one of the leading newspapers in Japan, had an article on the invasion of Hong Kong. It said:

"Mr. Majima is safe and the family feels relieved and happy about the news." But in fact, Mrs. Majima was out and the reporter did not interview her. When she came home the neighbours congratulated her. "Oh, really?" was her reply. She was not even concerned about her husband's safety. It would have been a long journey for a reporter to come from the centre of the city to Kyodo, so he just wrote down what a family would feel in a case like this. Ever since, I have never trusted what was reported in newspapers.

Across the street was an older house. The land in this Setagaya area was once very cheap. I think it was 50 yen a "tsubo" (3.306 square meters). So people who wanted a big house for very little money, bought land here and built big houses. Hence, some of the houses were quite big. The house across the street was one of those houses.

I forgot what kind of occupation the master of the Haruno family had. There were quite a number of children. The wife was a thin woman, who seemed to have no crispness in her body and spoke in a soft voice. One of the older daughters studied singing at a music conservatory of a lesser standing. Her voice did sound trained. But she was an object of ridicule by the mother of my classmate, Uno. Uno's family lived in the vicinity. They were not well off enough to send their daughter to good music teachers, so I think they were jealous of the Haruno's daughter. Uno's mother kept on telling us how bad Miss Haruno's voice was and how ridiculous it was for her even to think of entering a competition. The Haruno's youngest daughter was the same age as my younger sister and they entered the same elementary school together.

One day, Mrs. Haruno appeared in our entryway. She smiled and asked my mother if she could borrow some soy sauce. Whether she was oblivious of the fact that soy sauce was rationed and if the Harunos did not have it, we would not have it either or at least we would not have enough to share with other people, or she pretended not to notice it, I don't know. All I could think was how strange and stupid she was. I think my mother lent her (because she said she wanted to borrow; I don't think she had any intention of returning it) a spoonful. To our surprise she came again. This time she wanted to borrow sugar. I think, my mother, despite her weak spine, told her that we simply couldn't do it. There was absolutely none to spare.

She was not the only one who wanted to borrow things. Mrs. No, who was poor and could not afford to buy anything on the black market, could not heat water for a bath at home. All the public bathhouses had closed down for lack of fuel. My mother managed to get some fuel at black market prices and we were able to have a bath twice a week or so. Mrs. No was anxious to be invited over to our house so she could have a bath.

A Japanese bath is different from a Western style bath. One boils water in a big wooden tub. It is placed on concrete floor which has a drain. There is also a wooden board for the bather to squat and wash oneself. First, one scoops some hot water with a wooden basin from the tub and rinses oneself and then gets in the tub. After one is warmed up enough, one gets out of the tub, washes oneself, rinses the soap off the body thoroughly and gets back in the tub to warm oneself again. Japanese bath water is far hotter than a Westerner's bath water and fuel is constantly added to keep the temperature of the water warm. But since we had to use the same bath water and a guest must be the first person to use it, I hated an outsider using our bath. Mrs. No obviously had no choice and felt desperate, but she also knew that my mother was a nice person and would not refuse. Even my mother did not invite her every time we had a bath, but I hated sharing the bath with an outsider.

We also had difficulty trying to hide what we were cooking. Unfortunately, it was very difficult. The Nos were so poor that they could not afford to buy anything at black market prices. It was almost impossible for us to grill fish without having the smell travel to the next door. As soon as the first whiff of fish smoke hit the neighbourhood, Mrs. No's modest graceful face would peep between the bamboo sticks of the fence.

"My, what a delicious smell!" Thus a piece of fish had to be presented to her. In order to be fair, I am quite sure she would never have done any of the things she was doing had she not been compelled by poverty to do so. In return, she gave us, my elder sister and me, some jewellery, a remnant of the Nos' past glory: a rose stone necklace, broaches of semi-precious stones, and ornaments made of ivory.

At the start of the War, the government ordered the citizens to organize neighbours into groups, called "Tonarigumi" (a sort of block watch). Our neighbourhood was grouped into one with Mrs. Sugita as its head. Now, the head of the Tonarigumi had the duty to inform the members when the rationed rice was arriving at the store, when the rationed sweets were available, give instructions on how to make a padded hood to protect our precious heads in case of bombing, and pass on general information given by the government. Such information came on a clipboard and each one would place a seal after they had read it and pass it on to the next neighbour. The duty of taking it to the neighbour fell, as usual, on me. To my mother's sorrow, the duty of attending the meetings now and then could not have been passed on to me. I was too young, then, to attend such meetings.

This Tonarigumi system was a great breeding ground of gossip. One just could not keep one's privacy, which obviously was the purpose of the government. My mother hated it. But it was very important to keep up cordial relationships with the head of the Tonarigumi, for if one fell out of favour, one would be ostracized and would not get important information about when to get rice. Since my father was Korean, we were extra careful.

Mrs. Sugita coveted our ration tickets of sake and tobacco. My father neither smoked nor drank. Mrs. Sugita almost drooled over them. Of course, my mother was more than happy to present them to her—anything to buy the favour of the head of Tonarigumi. All middle-aged housewives in those days loved to talk and Mrs. Sugita was one of them. She would come unannounced and take a seat in the entryway and yap. One day, my mother found out a wonderful secret.

Mrs. Sugita came as usual, but before she sat down and made herself comfortable, she whispered into my mother's ear: "Is your second daughter in?" My mother, who did not know the reason why she asked, answered: "Yes." To my mother's surprise Mrs. Sugita said: "In that case, I shall come some other time." I was only twelve years old. But apparently she was afraid of me. She sensed my contempt for middle-aged women who did nothing but yak. Since that time, whenever we heard the front door open, I would go out to greet the visitor. Mrs. Sugita did not linger when she saw me but simply handed me whatever she had brought.

It was during this time that I became determined to go to university and get a higher education. Women were not admitted to universities and I didn't know how I was going to go to a university but I was going to do it. I was never, never going to be like one of those women I saw around me.

While we were in this house, Japan declared war on the U.S.A. It is a mystery why the thirteen men who sat around the table with Emperor Hirohito, to discuss the possibility of war with America, decided to declare war on the U.S.A. The emperor, who was a pacifist, asked for the opinion of the council and the Minister of the Navy answered that the navy had enough resources to fight for a year but after that it could not guarantee anything. The prime minister, who was a military general, went ahead and declared war on the U.S.A. The Japanese military believed they could beat America in two months. They were also dazzled by the initial successes of Nazi Germany under Hitler. They did not want to miss the wagon. As one can see, by studying history, many countries fell into the hands of maniacs or fools.

At the news of the declaration of war, my mouth hung wide open. At school, one of my classmates said to me: "Whatever is going to happen to Japan?" Even girls of thirteen or fourteen knew that this was the greatest folly Japan had committed but the adults in whose hands the fate of Japan rested didn't care.

My father was again in China. My mother and we, children, went downtown frequently in search of food. There was a famous fruit parlour, called Nishimura. The shop was open and served, since there was nothing else to sell, shaved ice cones. This was the only available food, so we ate a lot of it. Our stomachs, which had been weakened by the lack of proper food, got sick from the large consumption of ice. My elder sister was least affected. But my younger sister, Keiko, and I ended up in a hospital.

The day I got sick, I was at school. I got permission from the teacher to be dismissed and started for home. There was no taxi to be called so I walked. From the school to the house, it took at least half an hour. In the middle of the road I sat down several times because I felt an attack of diarrhea coming on and I did not want to make a mess. The doctor ordered us to go to the hospital.

My mother used to worry about not having savings so she saved carefully. But as soon as the amount got to 200 Yen, there would be an urgent need for the money and it would be gone. When we got sick, the amount was just about 200 Yen and, of course, it had to be spent on our medical care. Even the hospital was short of materials and the nurses were hungry, so my mother had to run around to get some cookies for the nurses. She was afraid that her children would not be looked after properly if she did not feed the nurses.

My mother also had a suitcase into which she tucked away bars of soap, quinine (because soldiers and civilians working in China or southeast Asia started bringing back to Japan the kinds of diseases which had not existed in Japan before), towels and other things. But this suitcase was lost in the post-war turmoil, even before we could use any of the items. She then realized that hoarding would not work and gave up the idea completely. In my opinion, if a portion of the money is not used for God, one will eventually lose the whole that one has diligently saved. There have been many examples where one has lost one's life savings when a portion was not dedicated to God first.

Now that food had disappeared completely from the shops and we were constantly hungry, all my classmates and I could talk about was food. We were obsessed with food. There were certain families who had connections with the higher ranks of the military and they could get food, but plain common folks had no such luck. The poor mothers, who had to find food, cook it with charcoals in a brazier, line up for hours to procure the necessities of life and had little money, were all in a bad mood.

Michiko, who used to be at the top of my class, once said to me: "My mother was so mad yesterday. She came home from an outing and said: 'You haven't even made tea for me.' She was really mad!" Her mother, who had spent hours out, must have been frustrated to find no tea waiting for her when she got back. In those days, one couldn't just turn on gas and boil water. One had to build a fire in a charcoal brazier as follows: one had to place paper, which was scarce, in the brazier, some kindling wood and finally charcoal. Since everything was made of material of a lesser quality, the charcoal did not catch fire so easily. It took a long time even to make tea.

Another girl, Terada, said: "My mother was hysterical last night. She was mad at me. She said: 'I will never help you again with your sewing'." Well, this was a very serious threat because most of us solicited our mothers' help for sewing from time to time.

Much to the chagrin of the principal, the school was ordered to have military training. A male soldier came to give us instructions on some military tactics, including sending signals with flags. I wanted to use "SOS" as frequently as possible. He made us march five kilometers on our empty stomachs. I was busy conjuring up various reasons how not to participate in the training. I was the tallest girl in our class and I always had to lead, but I was such a klutz that I wanted to avoid being at the head of the column. Since I was half Korean and did not take Japan's so-called cause seriously, my conscience was clear. All I wanted was a quick ending to the War.

A woman teacher of "Naginata" (a long spear with a half-moon shaped blade at the end made for use by women) was brought in to teach us how to defend ourselves in case the enemy landed on our soil. The Naginata we used were mock and made of wood. As we thrust a Naginata towards the enemy, we had to call out: "Eiya To". I don't know how useful this would have been towards the B29s that were flying over our heads. I am sure American pilots would have heard us and been scared.

As soon as we started the lesson, one of the girls told me that this cry was very bad for the vocal cords. It spoiled our singing. So I immediately stopped calling out loud and just shaped my mouth in the form of the outcry and acted generally like a fish that was short of breath. Only when the teacher came around did I use my voice.

The teacher was truly imbued with patriotic passion. Her strict serious face told me that she firmly believed that Japan was fighting for a just cause. I tried to beg off from this class as often as I could. But one day she was fed up with the number of absentees and gave a sermon in a solemn voice: "I have never been to a school like this where there are so many absentees from Naginata class! Too much Americanism exists in this school. Even the princesses of the Imperial family are never absent from Naginata class. Shame on you!" The whole class became deathly silent. Everyone's eyes were downcast and staring at the floor of the gym except mine.

Pleased with the effect of her sermon, she shouted: "Now the class will begin!" I raised my hand. "Excuse me, Miss ____ I would like to be excused from the class. I have a bit of a stomachache." Like an echo, she said without hesitation: "Yes, you may." I think her answer was so quick because she believed it. Since it was only a few minutes after her lecture, she could not believe that anybody would dare defy her words. I sat alone on the platform watching the class. When one of my classmates raised her eyes, I stuck out my tongue.

With the war going on around me and being forced to do things against my will, I sought refuge in something spiritual. Our school was giving us enough Bible reading and prayer hours, but I wanted more. I wanted to go to a church—a proper church. After some research, I selected the church at Aoyama Gakuin.

Aiko's Journey

This was the school where my sister first wanted to go and did not. The campus of this school was big because the school consisted of classes from kindergarten to post-secondary. They also had a nice old chapel on the campus. To get to the service on Sunday, I had to get up early in the morning, walk to the station, take a commuter train and then transfer to another line. I don't know how I did it; I can't remember. How I made breakfast or whether my mother made me breakfast or if there was anything to eat at all, I have no recollection. All I can remember was, I was there on Sunday and attended the service.

The Sunday school teacher was a young woman in her early twenties. From where I was standing, she looked very mature. She was wearing a sombre blue dress and looked very modest and Christian. On January 7, 1942, she gave a New Year's party at her home. Since I loved parties and became very animated at such functions, I was delighted and had a great time. We played "Sugoroku" (similar to monopoly), "Hyakunin Isshu" (one hundred Japanese waka, Japanese poems) and other similar games which were unique to New Year celebrations. I was also surprised to see food. She served us dumplings, rice crackers and mandarin oranges. I wondered inwardly how the family managed to get the food, but soon I immersed myself in playing games and eating. I went home flushed with pleasure and excitement.

Towards the early hours of the morning, I woke up with a peculiar sensation between my thighs. I tried to ignore it at first, but it would not go away. I got up and went to the toilet. I saw blood. I had become a woman.

chapter XIII

We moved again. This time, to a faraway place: Peking, China. The conditions in Japan were getting very bad. My father, who missed his family, wanted to take us to Peking where the conditions were better.

To move one whole household from Japan to a foreign country during the War, was a major operation. Since there was no means of transporting anything, we had to get rid of almost everything except the bare necessities. These bare necessities had to be carried by hand.

The greatest problem was the hygiene of the three women, who had monthly cycles: my mother, my sister and me. Since things were scarce, most women were washing absorbent cotton or rags after each use and were using them over and over again. We could not simply throw them away because there were no replacements. This meant we had to have a supply of such material for one week and had to carry them after they got dirty until we got to a place where we could use water. Not only that, in a crowded train where people would be sitting in the toilet, one could not even find a place to change. Very unfortunately, this thing invariably comes when you take a trip. At least it came for me on the day of our departure. I don't know how I solved this problem being a young girl of thirteen. But I managed without an accident.

On the ferry between Japan and Korea, I could not enjoy the sea as I did when I went to Korea. The Japanese military Government was afraid of espionage, so we were not allowed to be on the deck. So I had to stay downstairs with all the people around me getting seasick.

Once we crossed the border to Manchuria, an entirely different world stretched before us. Since the Russians built the Manchurian railroad, the tracks were wider than the Japanese ones and the trains had a different feel. . During the Russo-Japanese War of 1904-1905, the Russians destroyed the tracks as they retreated and the Japanese discovered that they could not replace them because the factories in Japan had no facility to produce rails for wide tracks. I rode the trains from Pusan to Peking twice and from Peking to Pusan once. Even now I love the recollection of these trips.

Unlike Japan which consists of four small islands, the Continent was a vast stretch of plains. The train ran stoically towards its destination. Outside the windows, miles and miles of flat land stretched out. All of a sudden there would be a tree, a puddle and a mud house and a little Chinese girl would stand there, waving and smiling. The Chinese have a tremendous life force. Where they got their daily supplies or where they got the clothes that the girl was wearing, I wonder even unto this day.

It took three days and two nights on the train to get to Peking. During the night, the light in the train was dimmed and all the shades were pulled down so that the train would be as invisible as possible and not be attacked by the bandits called the Paro (written in Chinese characters as Eight Roads) who were the rebels led by Mao Tse Tong against General Chang's government. They later became the communist government. But while the Japanese were invading China, both the Paro and General Chang's government agreed to collaborate with each other and fight against their common enemy, namely Japan.

The only light that shone in this vast empty land was the headlamp of the train. Inside the carriages, the light was so dim that once the evening came, there was nothing for the passengers to do. It was too dark to read, do any handiwork or play chess. At any rate, there would not have been any space in the luggage to put such things. We sat in our seats, staring at the faces in front of us, swaying to the movement of the train.

When we finally arrived, the city of Peking was shining in the strong summer sun of China. The brilliant red of Tiananmen Square greeted us.

But as soon as we stepped out of the station, we had the first taste of an entirely foreign culture. We were surrounded by a barrage of "yancho" (the Chinese version of a rickshaw) coolies. My mother was almost frightened when she was surrounded by the Chinese coolies with their skin darkened by the constant exposure to the strong sun, wearing blue cotton pants and a vest and speaking in a foreign language. We quickly had to learn the phrase: "Puyo" which meant "We don't need it". The competition among yancho men was fierce. Somehow we managed to select four: one for each of us, except for my younger sister, who rode with my mother. We headed for one of the European style hotels. Since anti-Japanese feelings were strong, we had to be careful that one of us would not be taken to a place where we did not intend to go.

At the hotel my elder sister and I were given a room. We were delighted to see Western style beds and we frolicked on them, feeling rather modern. This was a nice escape from drab Japan where everything was getting to be gloomy. After settling down, one of my father's colleagues invited us to a dinner at a Chinese restaurant. But before the dinner was put on the table, I wanted to go to the toilet. One of the men working at the restaurant led me to a room and gave me a night pot.

Many Chinese households did not have a proper toilet. They all used night pots. Since it did not rain often in China and the air is dry, the night soils dry up soon. But this was my first encounter with a night pot. I stared at it not knowing what to do. The window was open and I could see someone across the courtyard, a man facing my way, laughing.

I went back to the room where everyone was waiting for the dinner and told my father that I had to go back to the hotel. I could not explain to him why. I just insisted that I could not stay. My father was getting impatient and tried to persuade me to stay. I just kept on saying I couldn't. I can't remember what happened after that. I did not stay for the food for sure. I was sorry I spoiled the kindness of his colleagues and was sorry to miss the food. Even unto this day I do not visit countries where toilet facilities are not good. I don't care how wonderful the culture of this country is; I can't appreciate it if I am worried about the toilet facilities. One can live without looking at famous historical monuments (one can't see everything in the world anyway) but one can't survive without a proper clean toilet.

The next morning, the hotel served us porridge for breakfast. I did not quite appreciate the merit of this British custom. I tasted only a little bit of this gooey stuff. After a few days, my father moved us to a company house.

A Chinese house consists of several separate compounds with a courtyard in the middle. If it is a wealthy man's house, there are multiple compounds: one small compound with a courtyard near the entrance and another compound, separated by a gate, and so on. Tall walls would enclose several compounds and a beautifully-landscaped garden. The Chinese have a large scale for everything, so sometimes one household's walls would stretch for miles and the walls had gates in all four corners. Once one gets into a house like that, one would not be able to get out without someone guiding him as it would be like a maze inside. If a house was not that large-scaled, it at least had two compounds within the walls and one solid gate. If one wanted the gate to be opened, one had to use the metal knocker on the gate until someone heard you and would open the gate. If a household could afford servants, there would be a porter at the gate who would answer the calls. The visitor had to tip the porter. My mother, who was used to tipping, tipped porters generously so she was always shown in, but my father's superior's wife did not understand the way of life in China, so the master was always absent and could not see her.

The company house we moved to had only two compounds that faced each other with a small courtyard in between. In the house opposite, lived another family from the same company, but the man had a lower rank than my father. We certainly did not have the same lifestyle. They had a nineteen-year-old son who had been studying in Japan. But at that time, he had come home and was idle because he had contracted TB. Out of despair, he had developed a mean character. His mother was unhappy about her marriage and her son's illness. They also had a badly-brought-up brat who was about five years old.

The mother and her son both wanted to spend the day coming over to our side of the house to chat. We did not like the eldest son coming over because as he was in the last stage of TB, the illness was obviously highly infectious. But we could not tell him not to come. We especially abhorred the visit of the brat. The child's feet were always dirty and as soon as he came in, his footprints made marks on the wooden floor that my mother had polished so diligently. He came like a tornado always wanting to eat from our cupboard and making our lives miserable. His mother never made any effort to stop his coming. She was obviously pleased to be able to use us as free babysitters because that gave her a respite from her miserable life.

I think one main reason why Japanese wives were unhappy was that their husbands ignored them and had fun only by themselves; whereas, my father always took the whole family out, and we all shared in the fun. Those wives were never invited to Chinese restaurants or to visit famous sites, so they led a boring life, even in a foreign country where they could have enjoyed something different from their own culture. The Japanese in those days were not so open to learning about a new culture, either. They believed in the superiority of their race and looked down on everybody else. Since our father was Korean, we certainly did not believe in the superiority of any race and were more open to other cultures.

One afternoon the sky suddenly turned yellow.

"Mrs. Morimoto, close the shutters of the windows! Quick! Shut the door! Hurry up!"

It was the nineteen-year-old who was shouting. We sensed that something terrible was happening, judging from the colour of the sky, so we did as we were told. We firmly closed all the shutters and the door. Then it came. The sand storm, which had travelled across the plains of China all the way from Mongolia, arrived with the fierce force of nature. The wind screamed and rattled the openings of the house as if trying to get in. It raged over the city for about twenty minutes. We sat in the fetus position with our eyes closed, not wanting to look up or move. We were rigid with fear.

The storm passed and went away. It became quiet as if nothing had happened. But it left a souvenir of inches of rough sand throughout the whole house. Everything was covered with sand and we could not get rid of it for a long time. We were warned, then, that we should take refuge in any shop when we sensed a storm coming. But with a strong anti-Japanese feeling among the Chinese people, we were not quite sure which would be safer, the storm or inside a Chinese shop with the doors and windows closed.

The poor nineteen-year-old died soon afterwards. My sister and I had gone back to Japan to continue our schooling by then but our mother told us later. My parents had moved from this house to another one, which was a better place, so she had not seen him for some time. One day, while she was walking in the street, this boy passed by on a yancho. Instead of just passing by, he stopped the yancho, got off it and came over to my mother. She was surprised to see him act so politely after he had been rather nasty to us. He took off his hat and said gently: "Obasan, I am leaving soon (he meant he was going back to Tokyo) so I would like to say 'good-bye'." My mother knew at once that he was dying. She knew that "leaving" meant leaving this world. When an unkind person suddenly turns nice and kind, it is often a sign that this person is dying.

"So are you going back to Japan? Good luck. Take care."

He bowed, put on his hat again, got on the yancho that was waiting for him and went away. My mother watched him disappear full of emotion since she knew she would not see him again.

Now, in those days, Peking was one of the most beautiful cities in the world. The tall walls surrounded the city. The tops of the walls were so wide that one could walk on them. Near the gate of the walls, the leaves of willow trees swayed gently in the evening breeze. The bells of the yanchos echoed melodiously. The shops that lined the main street, Wan Fu Ching, still carried luxury items such as Coty lipsticks, face powder and other cosmetics. For daily supplies, such as vegetables and meat, we went to Tong Tan Pairo, and for things like candies, jewellery and other small items, Tong An Shichang was the place to go.

To be in Tong An Shichang (Market of Eastern Peace) and out of the heat of summer was a pleasant experience. The market was covered and inside it was cool and smelt of earth. The piles of candies were almost spilling over, but not many people were buying them. Because of high inflation, people had no money. In the jewellery stores, jade and rosestones were shining in the light.

The most enticing store had glasses filled with juices of various colours. We were given strict instructions never to drink them. Water in China was scarce. It was not like in Japan, where one could get water almost anywhere by digging a well, and where a well-developed aqueduct system existed. In China, one often had to buy water, so the water in the juices could be days or weeks old. The Chinese stomach was geared to it, so they did not get sick so easily, but the Japanese stomach was not. We would have come down with severe stomach trouble. I so wanted to drink them. They looked so nice. I had to control myself and just look at them admiringly.

My father took us to many historical sites, except the royal palace. The palace that appears in the film "The Last Emperor" was situated outside the walls of the city. With anti-Japanese feeling running high, it was not considered safe to go outside of the city. Even within the walls, we did not venture out to certain quarters of the city, but stayed where the Japanese were clustered.

One of the places we visited was Pehai Park (Park of the Northern Sea). It is actually not a sea but an artificial lake that was created by an emperor. The emperor's first attempt was a failure. When the water gushed into this newly-created lake, it overflowed and swallowed up three thousand spectators who came to watch the memorable event. The next attempt was a success and this artificial lake still gives much pleasure to visitors.

As I often mention, the Chinese are large scaled people. One calls it a lake but it is more like a sea than a lake. One cannot see the end of the lake; it spreads far into the horizon and one is impressed thinking how much work must have gone into the construction of this huge lake. We used to stop at a teahouse and drink tea. Before we poured tea into the cups we filled the cups with a little bit of hot tea, twirled it and rinsed the cups first. I don't know how effective it was, but since the Chinese sense of hygiene was quite different from that of the Japanese, we were careful even it was simply a ritual. The park had many tall mature trees. It was quiet, serene and beautiful. Sitting at the table in the shade, looking out over the vast expanse of the grey water of the lake, while we sipped tea from Chinese teacups, was one of my memories to be treasured.

My father also took us to the countryside where he was actually

Aiko's Journey

working. The more remote the place where one worked, the more money one would get. So, quite a few Japanese, including women, were working there. It was the place where the coalmines were excavated. The Japanese, of course, did not go into the pits, the Chinese did. The Japanese were engaged in clerical jobs.

The women working there were like autumn leaves blown into a corner of an alley. They had to endure insults coming from men with no prospect of hope for the future. These were the days when women did not even have suffrage. Working women, who had passed marriageable age, were like garbage which men felt free to trample on. Women had to put up with insults heaped on them, phrases like: "You are only a woman" or "Why don't you act like a woman" or "If you act like that, you can't get married"(who wants to marry you?). The women working there were mature women so they had to put up with sexual innuendo and other various irritations coming from the men.

Having seen this desolate place, I realized how much sacrifice my father was making for us. There were absolutely no entertainment facilities, cultural events or educational centers. There was a canteen that served as a general store but the stock was poor, perhaps owing to the war. Some Japanese soldiers in their uniforms were hanging around, since this was a Japanese-occupied territory.

One day, when my mother, my sisters and I were walking down the road near the canteen, I saw a Japanese woman clad in a kimono standing with a Japanese soldier. The way she had the kimono on was quite different from the way my mother wore hers. The kimono was made of cheap material and the obi (the sash) was flat. The whole outfit looked loose and the woman definitely did not seem to belong to the "housewives' club". I called for my mother's attention.

"Who is that woman?" My mother did not answer me but quickened her pace. She did not even look at the woman.

"You don't have to know," she said curtly. She was one of the comfort women, who went to work in remote places like this in order to earn more money. All of the women working in this job were strapped with large amounts of debts and they were always seeking the opportunity to earn more money.

One evening, we went for a walk. We strolled down a desolate open area dotted with Chinese houses where the Chinese laborers lived. In one of the houses, I could see a woman tidying up a room. Her black hair was pulled back and tied in a knot. I could see the earthen floor and a bare room. As we walked, a tiny human dot was coming towards us. When we came closer, we discovered that it was a little Chinese boy. He wore traditional Chinese clothes and shoes and was carrying a basket on his back. It was the kind of basket a miner would carry coals in. We all felt pity for him. He was such a forlorn and sad figure.

My father asked him in Chinese: "How old are you?"

"Seven" was the answer. Now this was the Chinese seven. So according to the Western calculation, it would have been about five and half. My father said some more nice things in Chinese. We wanted to take him home and save him from this hard labour of carrying coals on such a tiny back. He nodded and plodded on. We had to turn around several times to have another look at him.

"Such a small child", my father said with emotion. Our hearts were heavy, knowing that we could not help him. The sad life of another human being bit my heart. The emotion was so intense that it did not even induce tears. In the evening I entered in my journal: "This child would never know about Chopin's music or any other niceties of life." I knew how much more blessed my life was.

In the vicinity, there were very old and famous carvings in the rocks. My father wanted to take us there. But since one had to ride in an open truck on bumpy country roads, only three of us, my father, my elder sister and I, went. I enjoyed sitting in the back of the speeding truck with the summer sun pouring down and my hair blowing in the breeze. The carvings in the rock were a part of the ancient history of China. Unlike most of the Japanese at the time, my mind was not closed to different cultures and I was impressed by their magnificence.

Afterwards, we went to see the spring which supplied the water for Peking. The pristine water that sprang out of the rocks and poured into the river was not at all like the brown water we were getting in the city of Peking. Although the water that was springing out was pure, clear and beautiful, we could not drink it without boiling it, because even as we were looking on, women were washing their clothes and kitchen utensils in the pure serene water. As water was scarce, this water had to travel miles and miles to Peking in pipes (in those days, the quality of the pipes was different from that of today), and by the time it got to the city, it was brown and had no resemblance to the clear water we saw at the source.

My mother and my younger sister had returned to Peking earlier and my elder sister and I were to follow later. Soon after they left, an alarm was sounded. The Paros were attacking the next village. We were to gather in a certain place. The men went out to guard the outside. Inside a small room, women sat crammed together and scared. Strangely enough, I was not scared. Having experienced war more closely in Tokyo, I was rather calm. However, the Chinese soldiers actually descending upon us would have been different. I somehow felt we would be spared from the raid.

One of the women was actually trembling. She was obviously thinking of being raped and dragged away to a remote village. She was, at the time about twenty-seven, long past marriageable age and very unhappy. Long years of struggle made her a brash woman. She was not very big but her features were strong and she stood out more than other women. So, if any soldier were to kidnap a Japanese woman, she would have been the first target. She also had a defiant attitude, without which, she would not have survived in this male-dominated society. It struck me as strange, therefore, to see this otherwise strong woman be so afraid and timid. Very fortunately we were soon told that the Paros, after having raided the next village, retreated and we were free to go home.

My elder sister and I were to return to Peking to get ready for school that would start in September. A young Korean man was going to accompany us. In the train, we must have been in the third class because a lot of Chinese shared the compartment. I remember particularly one woman who came in with a rolled-up comforter. She was about forty years old, obviously belonging to a poor peasant class, and wearing a blue Chinese jacket and blue pants. What attracted my attention were her eyes. She had her head downcast and was wiping her eyes with a piece of cloth. I knew at once that she was suffering from trachoma. I watched her take the dirty cloth to her eyes to wipe away the pus that was constantly corning out of them and my heart ached. It was quite clear that the use of that dirty cloth just aggravated the disease and, without proper treatment, she would soon be blind. At our elementary school in Japan, we had regular physical check-ups and trachoma, which was quite rampant in those days, was immediately treated. This was China in 1942. I could not keep my eyes off her, saddened by her fate.

When we got to the station in Peking, Japanese soldiers inspected our suitcases. There may have been some incident to cause this precaution. Coarse army soldiers made the travellers open their suitcases and their rough hands groped among our things. One soldier came over to us and ran his fingers through our clothes. We cringed at his act. He then very unfortunately grabbed the package we had hidden under the clothes. The package had old clothes we used for sanitary purposes in it.

"What's this?" he shouted and proceeded to open it in public. The Korean fellow who accompanied us was standing behind us with a cool face. Since he was Korean, he did not like the Japanese and obviously had contempt for such a barbarous act. He solemnly opened his mouth.

"This is something only ladies need."

I could almost hear the soldier gasp. He quickly threw the package back into the suitcase and said: "Go away. Hurry up." These were the days when men and women were modest around each other. If the soldier had felt embarrassed, we young girls felt ten times more so. We could not raise our faces.

When we got back to Peking, my elder sister and I had to go to the Japanese joggakko (girls school) and register ourselves. There was only one in the whole city. My mother accompanied us. There was a bustle of young girls in the school and while we were standing in the hallway, we heard someone call out in a loud voice: "Red skirt!" Coming from Tokyo and attending a school where there were many people who had a lot to do either with Europe or the United States of America, we were quite westernized in the way we wore clothes. So on that day I was wearing a red skirt that was made by a dressmaker who had studied in the U.S.A. The Japanese who were in China in those days firmly believed in the superiority of their race and were convinced that their just cause (that Japan would unite Asia into one and would become its leader) would win. To such a mentality, I, in a modern red skirt, was an object of ridicule and a sign that I was not serious about the War. I was a traitor. I realized for the first time how the ordinary Japanese, without God's teaching and a wide perspective, would act.

I must admit that the teacher who took us around was nice. She was about forty (maybe younger but in those days women looked more mature than today), had her hair pulled back in a bun, wore a white shirt blouse and a blue skirt, which was a standard teacher's outfit, and spoke nicely and kindly. My mother spent a considerable amount of money purchasing our school textbooks. Then we got a sheet of paper upon which the school rules were written. We were astounded reading them.

For the first time my elder sister and I found out how a pure Japanese school functioned. It was a shock for us for we were used to Westernized liberal Christian ideas. I have forgotten most of the ridiculous rules but I still remember a few of them. One was, of course, not to wear Americanized outfits, such as the red skirt (how was this going to help win the War?), another was never to go to a cinema (a source of evil temptation) and another was never to ride a yancho. The Japanese, who had a true Japanese spirit, should not be so weak as to ride a yancho but should walk. This also was a ludicrous idea for us, who were used to the well-developed public transportation system in Tokyo. What would it add to the cause of the War if one walked from Shibuya (a station in Tokyo) to Nihonbashi (another station in Tokyo) aside from the fact that one is too pooped to work afterwards? As to being forbidden to go to the movies, how could anybody think up something so stupid? If a person has his or her own mind, this person can go to the movies six times a day and will not be corrupted. It is not an outside object that corrupts a person, but it is what is inside them. . I despised the rules and the narrow-minded stupidity.

But at least a Japanese school accepted my elder sister and me but my younger sister was not so lucky. On the day she was to register at the only elementary school in Peking, my father took her there. My elder sister and I were to go there and pick her up when the registration was finished. We went there around the time she should have finished. But we could not find her. We enquired at the office. The female clerk, when she found out we were Koreans, said to us in an uncaring, unkind, cold voice: "Oh, is she Korean? In that case she won't be here. We don't accept Korean children." She directed us to the Korean school. Neither my sister nor I was acquainted with the map of the city of Peking, but in our desperation we managed to get to the Korean school.

The building was far inferior to that of the Japanese school. The Japanese herded the Korean children in an extremely perfunctory manner. The inside of the classroom was dingy, the scholastic standard seemed much lower and the air of sadness of an oppressed people hung in the whole place. The children were reciting some Japanese text in subdued mumbling voices. Hatred against the unreasonable Japanese oppression sharply stabbed my heart. My younger sister was not there, either. We had to go home.

It was a long way. Tall walls of Chinese houses stood on both sides of the streets. It does not rain often in China but, as if to accompany our sorrows, the sky turned grey and rain started to fall. Both my sister and I began to cry. We had been used to hearing "Koreans are not accepted here", "You Korean?" or other derogatory remarks, but while we attended Keisen Jogakuen, we were spared such hurts. It stung us anew. The rain came down mercilessly. The rain in China is harsh and strong. My sister and I were not equipped for the change in the weather. Soon, the roads became pools of muddy water. As we ran, mud splashed onto our skirts and our tears mingled with the falling rain.

When we got home, we discovered that my father had brought my younger sister back home instead of taking her to the Korean school. He was too broken by the insult inflicted by the Japanese. The small bundle that was my younger sister was sitting in front of him, not fully grasping the meaning of it. When we saw them, we burst out crying. My father did not speak but when I looked up at his face, I saw tears sliding down his cheeks silently. I never saw him cry before nor afterwards.

My mother, as usual, put on her best kimono and looking nice, went to see the principal of the school. "I hear you do not accept Korean children. Is it not against what the Japanese preach?" demanded my mother.

"Oh, is it your child? In that case, of course, she is welcome."

The principal, who was impressed by a lovely Japanese woman, immediately accepted my younger sister. Besides my younger sister, there was another child who was not purely Japanese. It was a boy who was born to a Japanese woman, who was the fourth wife of a very wealthy Chinese man. She was a beautiful woman whom the Chinese costumes suited outstandingly. Normally a Japanese figure did not look nice in a Chinese costume but she was an exception. She looked extremely elegant in foreign costumes and carried herself like a wealthy man's wife.

My mother gave me the duty of overseeing my younger sister at school to make sure that she was not mistreated because she was half Korean. It was almost comical, when I think of it now, that a thirteen-year-old girl had tried to supervise a grown-up teacher, but my mother would not do it herself. The Chinese boy's beautiful mother also came to school to make sure that her boy was all right. We bowed to each other in acknowledgement.

The boy later came to school alone on his family's yancho. He looked more Chinese than Japanese because he wore rings on almost every finger. Japanese men would never wear rings, let alone on every finger. He used to say to my sister: "I am Japanese, am I not?" The school tolerated his rings maybe because of the influence of his father's money. At any rate, China, even with the Japanese occupation, was an independent country and they could not control the Chinese the same way they did the Koreans. I often wonder what happened to that beautiful woman and her boy after Japan lost the War and later when the communists came into power.

On the day my elder sister and I were to attend the school, we lugged our textbooks without using a yancho, keenly feeling the need to ride it. We went to our respective classrooms, ready to absorb knowledge. To our astonishment there was no teaching. I knew that some of the schools in Japan had given up teaching and sent their students to factories to work for the War, but since our old school did not believe in the War, the students were still in the classrooms studying. But this school in Peking was a pure Japanese school. None of the teachers had studied abroad and the Japanese in Peking believed in the just cause of the War. So to express their eagerness to participate in it, the students had ceased to waste time on such things as learning or acquiring abstract ideas.

However, unlike in Japan, there were no ammunition factories, nor any other place where these girls could work. So what they were doing was cleaning the floors of the classroom (which would take only one hour at most) and the rest of the time sitting around gossiping. I was appalled at the hypocritical inconsistency. If they had only floor cleaning to do, they might as well study something and gain some knowledge.

As I sat alone in a corner of the room, the rest of the girls clustered around a girl who seemed to be the boss and talked about others. I could hear the fragments of "So-and-so......", or "Nee....?" trying to get the others' agreement. Nobody invited me to join in (not that I wanted to join that kind of a group). But I had a faint hope of trying to be friendly and sent a feeble smile in that direction. The boss girl responded benevolently, but no invitation came. I was quite sure that the Japanese, who had such small hearts and this exclusive attitude, would not succeed in becoming the leader of the whole of Asia.

After three days of going to school and listening to useless yapping, my sister and I were fed up. We wanted to go back to the school in Tokyo. So we quit. My mother, who had spent a lot of money for the purchase of the textbooks, which never came into use, half laughed and half cried, thinking of the wasted money. We would have to be boarders at the school in Tokyo since the rest of the family would have to stay in Peking. We sat down and wrote a letter to Miss Kawai begging her to take us back and let us become boarders.

While we were waiting for a reply from Japan, we were freed from the rules and restrictions of the school in Peking; now that we were no longer their students. I wore my red skirt freely and looked down from the yancho on the students who were sweating in the late summer heat in their white shirts and blue serge skirts. (Their minds were so inflexible; they were wearing woolen serge skirts in Peking's boiling heat!)

The reply came. We would be accepted in the dormitory that was attached to the private residence of the principal of the school. This was a great privilege because only the students who were personally connected to the principal were invited to live there. I think Miss K wanted to show special love for us since we were Koreans.

The journey back to Tokyo would be difficult and complicated. Since one could no longer buy daily necessities in Tokyo, we had to buy in Peking such things as a washbasin, soap, towels, underwear, winter clothes and summer clothes, and lug them back to Tokyo. We could not send them through the post or by express. If we had done so, there was no way of telling how long it would take or, for that matter, if they would ever arrive safely at the designated address. Added to this already-heavy luggage, we had to carry enough food for three days. How could we keep the food from spoiling in the heat? We didn't want to think.

On the day of departure, my father came to see us off at the train station with my younger sister. Anticipating the difficulty that lay ahead of us, his face had an inexplicable expression. After all, my elder sister had just turned fifteen and I was still thirteen. We had to journey all the way to Japan surrounded by tough adult men. Added to that, my sister, who was supposed to have proper identification papers as she had turned fifteen, did not have them. My father purposefully did not get them. We looked Japanese (to the Japanese) and our speech was perfect. We did not have to call unnecessary attention to the fact that we were Koreans. Without looking at the papers, they would not know. We, too, knew that we should risk it and leave our fate to heaven, which we were convinced, was on our side and not on the side of the persecuting Japanese. My father said simply: "Be careful."

Soon the train pulled out of the station, leaving my father's worried look behind and two young children in the train. I would never forget that look on my father's face as long as I live. One of the men in the same compartment sensed the situation and I could tell that he wanted to play insidious tricks on the two defenseless girls. The train proceeded, indifferent to the various passengers' sentiments.

When it was time to eat, we took out our meager food supply. After a few bites, my sister sniffed it and said: "Don't eat it. I think it's gone bad." Since I was known to stuff myself with any kind of food regardless of the condition it was in and my sister was known to know the condition the food was in, I meekly followed her instruction and threw away the food. My heart went with it. There was nothing else to eat. At one station I saw a Chinese vendor passing by the window with a whole roasted chicken upon his head. The saliva flowed in my mouth and my stomach growled. After that, we did not eat properly for three whole days.

At some point, my sister managed to buy two cones of ice cream. The ice cream looked more like condensed dirty water. I lapped it eagerly but again my sister grabbed it out of my hand. "This is cheap stuff. It will give us a stomachache (which would have been true). Don't eat it." I threw it away grudgingly. The nasty man was licking his ice cream without any reservation. I knew that he, coming from a tough class, would have a tougher stomach and would most likely not get sick. He clicked his tongue ostentatiously, saying: "Hm. It's yummy." I glared at him wishing him evil.

Just before the train reached the border between Manchuria and Korea, a government official came in to check our ID papers. My sister and I put on an innocent look. He stood in the aisle and said: "May I see your papers?" We handed him our train season passes. He looked at the passes with pictures and us. Then he said to my sister: "How old are you?"

"Fifteen."

He twirled the passes in his hand. "Do you know that you have to have proper identification papers because you are fifteen?"

"On, my!", both my sister and I exclaimed with feigned surprised looks

"Do we have to get off here? Our father must have been ignorant of the fact. He didn't say anything. What shall we do?" We tried to look as distressed as we could.

"What is the purpose of the trip?"

"We are going back to the school in Tokyo."

We held our breath. After a few seconds of silence he smiled at us and said: "You may go on. Have a nice trip." And he left.

At the border of Manchuria and Korea we had to exchange money. The paper money issued in China or Manchuria would have been as valueless as plain paper once it was off the Continent. It had to be changed into Japanese currency. However, the train would stop at the station where the exchange wickets were located, for only a few minutes. There would be a deadly struggle among the passengers, who did not want to be left with the worthless money of the Continent.

My sister went out to the deck even before the train came into the station. She jumped off the train before it came to a halt. She used the skill our military training instilled in us and her young legs were able to outrun the middle-aged. I stuck my head out of the window, praying that she would make it. I could see the soldiers in their uniforms, middle-aged women and men scrambling to the wickets. My sister came back before anybody else, holding the Japanese money in her hand. We slumped down in the seats, overcome by the victory.

The train came into Pusan and we tried to book into the best hotel as my father had instructed us to do. The hotel was fully booked. My sister took out a five-Yen bill and tipped the front desk clerk. The only available space was a bathroom. We were shown into the tiny room and they provided us with some kind of bedding. It was fortunate that it was late summer and we did not need too many covers. I was so tired and hungry that I just collapsed into the bathtub which was going to be my bed. After a few hours of awkward sleep, we had to be up again because the ferry for Japan would be leaving early in the morning.

Before long, my sister woke me up. Even in an emergency like this, we faithfully washed our faces. Still half asleep and dragging our suitcases, we went to the ferry terminal. Since the military government was afraid of spies getting information about the condition of the port of Pusan, they had built tall wooden walls along the corridors which led us around the terminal like a labyrinth. So instead of being able to get on the ferry directly from the pier, we had to walk round and round until we finally got to the ferry boat.

This was a tough job even for grown-ups. I tried to carry my heavy suitcase that contained a washing bowl but my thirteen-year-old arm could not manage it. My sister tried to help me but even her strength was limited. I finally collapsed half crying onto the concrete floor together with my suitcase that contained a washing bowl. I heard the heavy footsteps of adults rushing by me but I could not get up. Just then I heard a male voice speak to me.

"Aren't you ladies Mr. Morimoto's daughters?" I nodded feebly.

"I am a colleague of your father's. Come on. I will help you. Get up. Hurry."

I picked myself up and followed the man, who was now carrying my suitcase as well as his. He was clad rather elegantly in a blue blazer and white pants, which made him look like an expatriate returning home. There was a flight of stairs, which I almost rolled down to catch up to the pace of the adults. But thanks to my father's colleague's help, we made it to the ferry boat.

But when we got to Shimonoseki, another shock was waiting for us. Since September is the typhoon season in Japan, there is often some kind of calamity, especially in the southern part of Japan. The typhoon had just hit the area near Shimonoseki and had washed away the railroad between Shimonoseki and Hiroshima. There would be no trains running and no one could tell how long the repair would take. My sister and I decided to check into a hotel and think. My sister left me at the station and went looking for a red cap. Too tired, I sat down on the dirty concrete floor. I learned, there and then, that human beings can survive without washing their hands with soap before each meal or worrying about germs. My mother's teachings about cleanliness went out of the window and I still did not get sick.

My sister came back with an older red cap. All young men had been drafted and were fighting at the front. We told him to take the suitcases to the exit of the station. But since I was a cautious type, I had looked at the number that was attached to his chest. Even unto this day, I often look at the name of the cab driver or look at the license number of other cars and memorize it. So this time, too, I looked at his chest and memorized the number. As soon as he took off with our luggage, my father's colleague came over to us hurriedly.

"They have announced that they will run a special ferry to Hiroshima. It will leave in ten minutes. Come quickly and reserve your seats." We started following him. Our hearts pounded worrying about our suitcases which were now on their way in the opposite direction. On the way, I stopped a red cap, who was standing around.

"Please tell the red cap with such-and-such a number to bring back our suitcases to the ferry at the pier. We are leaving for Hiroshima. Please, please, hurry!"

Although he went in search of him, we were not even sure whether or not he would succeed in locating him. We managed to get on the crowded ferry. As soon as we got on, the gong was sounded. I leaned over the rail of the deck and stretched my neck like a yearning crane. My sister went down to the gangway to receive the suitcases if they ever came. After the gong, the boat trembled slightly to separate itself from the pier and started slowly to move away. There appeared about ten centimeters of brown water between the boat and the pier.

Then we saw him. Since he was not that young, it took him longer to get to the ferry boat. But the red cap, to whom we had entrusted our message, did convey it. I saw our red cap bend his not-so-young hips and throw the suitcases onto the boat. My sister's hand with the payment barely touched his stretched-out hand. But the suitcases came back to us. We collapsed onto the floor with relief. One of them was the black suitcase my mother nearly lost in Korea. Years later when I got to the port of New York I left it standing on the pier and went off to stay with a friend in New Jersey, and the next day, I had to come back to retrieve it. It now sits in the storage room of my condominium without doing any mischief. I haven't had the heart to part with it.

The ferry soon accelerated up to speed. It was so crowded that there was no space for us to sit down. My sister tipped one of the stewards, but after a deep bow and words of thanks, he did not help us. We stayed on the deck with the others who could not find a cabin inside. Suddenly a bundle of pink appeared on the deck. Among the drab-looking, tired passengers, this colourful vision looked almost out of place. When my sister and I stared at this pink apparition, we noticed that this was one of the girls who went to the same school, Keisen. We knew that her family was well-off. She was obviously with her parents, and with her wealthy parents' protection, she had secured a proper cabin. She looked refreshed and she was wearing pink pyjamas and a pink dressing gown. Judging from her self-assured smile on her face, she made a special trip to the deck to show off her Western style night attire. I was struck by her consciousness of the subtle sexual allure of her feminine body. Compared with her, I was an ignorant bookworm child. She was younger than I was.

The ferryboat docked in Hiroshima the next day. The first thing my sister and I did was to march into the restaurant at the station and sit down at a table. I can't remember how we got any food without a ration coupon, but a waitress took our order of curried rice. One thing that struck me was the complete absence of male figures. I felt that the War must be in pretty bad shape. The waitress brought the curried rice. I was impressed by the white rice: the first I had seen since we left Peking, but the curry did not have a single piece of meat in it.

The train took us to Tokyo and we arrived at the dormitory safely with the suitcase that contained a washing bowl.

chapter XIV

A new life began.

At the dormitory, they put me in a room with three other girls. One girl was older and was studying horticulture at the junior college of Keisen. The school was known for horticulture, which was a rare subject to study in Japan in those days. Another girl was my sister's classmate and the youngest girl was one class below me. This was the first time that I was thrown into an environment where I had to live in such proximity with people with different backgrounds. Naturally, those who lived in the dormitory came from areas outside of Tokyo, so their lifestyles were a world apart from mine. We all had to put up with one another's irritating habits.

The older girl, who was studying horticulture, used to lie around on tatami mats, instead of sitting up. She would raise one leg high while she talked; I couldn't tell for what purpose. By doing so, she showed her originally-white-but-now-grey underpants freely. It was a torture for me to watch it.

My sister's classmate came from the area where people are known to be tight-fisted. Later, when we had to share the goodies sent by our parents, she never shared with us what she received from home, but freely took our offerings.

The youngest girl was nondescript but had a nice nature. My sister was lucky. She was placed in a Western style room that was only big enough for two girls. So she had only one roommate.

It is said that, whatever the situation one is placed in, it is a grinding stone for one's soul. Each place is where one learns what one does not know yet and through the learning, one becomes a better person. I think it is true. While I was at home, my mother let me read as much as I wanted to and left me alone when it concerned housekeeping duties. She more or less let me live my life the way I wanted to, and I had absolutely no knowledge of life skills.

When I started living in the dormitory, I did not even know how to dry a dish. We, girls had to take our turns helping in the kitchen, filling the bath, cleaning the toilet and other various miscellaneous tasks. The first time I had to help in the kitchen, I did not even know how to dry the dishes, so I just stood there holding a tea towel. But young girls are neither as loving nor as patient as my own mother, so I quickly had to learn many things. Having to wash in the morning with cold water was tough enough, but to clean the toilet with cold water was hard labour for a girl of thirteen. I thought this hell would never end.

I hate communal life at any rate. I was miserable because I was forced to live with others, who had different backgrounds and manners. The first shock I got the day after I arrived was that the girls casually trampled the "getas" (wooden thongs) that were placed at the entrance. At home, I would leave the getas in an orderly manner and we were not allowed to walk over them. But such consideration was thrown to the wind. The girls walked over them as if they were the floor, so the getas would go all over the place. My expensive getas, that I had placed neatly, were trampled over by dirty feet and kicked out of place in no time.

The young girls were all struggling to survive and did not have enough room to have consideration for others, and the younger ones at the lowest rung of the ladder suffered most. At around that age, one year made one much more mature and made life a little easier. The trouble with a group living like this is that the older girls have the power and authority to boss around the young ones, and yet, they have not acquired the generosity or understanding of adults that come with maturity.

They were two sisters from another city in China. Their father had a thriving business there, and the family was quite well off. The older of the sisters was going to the junior college, but from what I could see, she was not particularly interested in study. She was in the department that did not require too much studying (or it did but she did not make much effort) and was getting average marks. She was more interested in marrying the manager, who was working at her father's office, and settling down as a wife and a mother. Since she was a motherly type and quite a bit older than I, she did not go out of her way to be mean to me. If she was not overly benevolent, it was just because she was human and very young herself.

The greatest problem was her chatting. We, young ones were allowed to study in the dining room till 8:00 o'clock and after that, we had to retire to our bedrooms, where there was no light. All the girls were supposed to be studying in the dining room in SILENCE. After dinner, there was not much time left for us to study before 8:00 o'clock. During this precious hour, Nori would not stop talking. Holding the maid's baby in her arms, she would talk, talk, and talk. Actually, I summoned my courage once or twice and told her nicely that I could not study with her yapping going on. She apologized (she was good natured this way) and stopped talking, but it did not last long. She would soon resume chatting. It was just not in her character to study seriously. Finally I gave up and just sat there with the books open and my time wasted. When I got in my bed, I would cover my head with the blanket and study with a flashlight.

Studying with a flashlight was strictly forbidden, but it was an open secret among the girls; everyone was doing it. To believe that anybody could finish studying within the designated time was an optimistic delusion. Sometimes there would be a sudden inspection, but anybody who came around to check, would have found every girl sleeping with her eyes closed and face turned towards the ceiling. As soon as the inspector left, we resumed our studying with the flashlight. The quality of the batteries was inferior, but batteries were still available. Since my bedroom was adjacent to the dining room, I could hear Nori's yapping for quite some time until she herself went to bed.

Nori's younger sister, Sachiko, was not only different in looks from her sister, but she was quite different in character. She was aggressive, strong and self-centered and had almost no consideration for others. She had brought beautiful cotton dresses from home—a lot of them. One day she invited my sister and me to her room to view her dresses. She brought from the cupboard an armful of dresses and hurled them onto the bed. (The building we were living in was originally a Western-style house which was converted into the living quarters for the girls; therefore, some of the rooms were still Western style with Western beds.) The dresses spread out like colourful flowers. I, who was used to having only two dresses, just had to admire the number and the beauty of them.

On Sunday, we were sent to a church outside of the school. Sachiko could not make up her mind which dress to wear. Despite the fact she had so many dresses and was from a family that could afford them, she liberally borrowed other people's things. She casually wore my getas without my permission and I hated it. The top board of wood of a geta is supported by two small pieces of wood. The bottom part of the geta diminishes in a certain manner depending on who is wearing them. When I wore them, the wooden pieces diminished evenly, but when Sachiko wore them, they became uneven after one wearing. The top wood became greasy from her perspiration. Replacements were difficult to find due to the shortages caused by the War. At any rate, a new pair would have suffered the same fate.

The other thing she wanted to borrow was my fountain pen. I had a pen with a gold nib and she often wanted to borrow it. When she returned it, though, the nib was all crooked and I could no longer write with it. She aggressively pressed the nib onto the paper. I took it to a stationery store nearby to have the nib changed. The proprietor of the shop had a smarmy smile and I later found out why. My mother discovered the following summer what he had done and we were struck by the dirty trick he had played on a young child. He took the gold nib and replaced it with another made of cheap metal.

The majority of the girls were afraid of Sachiko and it would have been untrue if I said I was not afraid of her. I had a fear of her because she was so self-centred that she would make a fuss if anything happened to her, while she would do exactly the same thing to others. She would order around the younger ones freely but she would not do anything for them.

One day, she was in the group that was in charge of the kitchen. She was supposed to get the items necessary for cooking, but she forgot to get one of them. If any of us had done that, she would have shouted at the top of her voice accusingly, but since it was she herself who forgot, she was quiet. But she didn't want to take the trouble of going out again to get it herself. So she came to my door and knocked.

"Mi-chan, can you go and get it?" she said in a coaxing voice. I was fed up with her selfish attitude. Something in me snapped and I said strongly, "No". If I had been in her position, would she go out and help me? No, she would be the last person to do it for me. My independent spirit spoke up.

"No, I can't go. I am studying now." Inwardly I was scared but I kept a brave front. As I expected, she screamed on the top of her voice. Her coaxing voice was gone.

"That's all right, then."

She banged the door so hard that it shook. I sat there holding on to the desk. I would not give in. I was a bit scared that she might retaliate but, as is often the case with people of that kind, a blow up took care of it, though she did pout and glare at me later, for a while.

My sister reacted differently to our new circumstances. The first thing she worried about was the shortage of our clothes. Especially after she had seen Sachiko's dresses, she seemed to have keenly felt the fact that we each had only two dresses. I didn't care how many outfits we had. I came back to study, so studying was my first priority. I wasn't envious of what Sachiko had. That was her business. My purpose in life was not the same as hers. But my sister made efforts to seek out a dressmaker in the neighborhood and have her make blouses and skirts. I followed her reluctantly to the shop. I did not like her preoccupation about our external image. But in personal relationships, she, unlike me, got along well with others because she had inherited more of the Japanese temperament and did not ruffle any feathers. She was more obedient and was not independent in spirit like me.

But my sister, being the elder of the two, protected me as much as she could. For instance, since there was a shortage of food generally, our meals were rationed and we were always hungry. From time to time, one of the boarders got a package from home and if the girl was generous, she would share the contents with her roommates. In our room, K. never shared her package while she would gladly partake in others'. The maid, Toku, sometimes got hold of extra food and invited a few of her favorite girls to sneak into her room late at night to taste it. If she had invited all of us, there wouldn't have been enough to go around, so she could not be blamed for not inviting the whole house. My sister got on the list for special treatment and took me along. I would not have managed it if I had been alone because I was too obnoxious and unique to be liked by those kinds of people.

Now it was strictly forbidden for us to take a nap during the day. But my sister was the kind of person who needed a nap from time to time. So one afternoon, she crept into the bed (she was in a Western style room) and fell asleep. Suddenly, without warning, the principal walked in, carrying a toolbox. There was something in the room that needed repair. My sister had no time to jump out of the bed so she slipped into the bed more deeply, covered her head and made herself flat. My sister was not exactly a person we would call skinny but in desperation, she tried. Miss K. placed her toolbox right on my sister, quite ignorant of the fact that there was a human being lying underneath. My sister's roommate wanted to laugh but suppressed the desire. The principal stayed in the room for about ten minutes, finished the repair and left. My sister emerged from under the covers and she and her roommate burst out laughing.

One of the tasks assigned to us at the dormitory was to draw the bath. The bathtub was the type, called "Goemonburo". Unlike other domestic bathtubs, this one was made of cast iron. The name "Goemon" was derived from the name of the infamous thief who, for his punishment, was boiled to death in this type of tub. The shape of the tub was round. Since the tub was made of iron, its sides and bottom could get really hot. There was a round-shaped wooden board meant to cover the bottom which would firstly float on the top of the water. The first person to take the bath was to stand on the top of the board and press it down to the bottom of the tub by her or his own weight. All the while the person has to support and balance herself or himself by holding on to the wooden rims around the tub. Since the wooden board was not yet soaked with water, it was light and tended to float. If one had not succeeded in pushing it down to the bottom and clicking it into the hook at the bottom, it would float back to the surface and hit one in the face, as if in revenge. If one did not lift one's feet quickly enough, one would have burned one's soles. But all of us were young and had enough agility and skill to avoid burning ourselves.

The girls took turns in pairs to have a bath. Once I took a bath with a junior college student and when I saw her naked body, I exclaimed: "My, you are dark skinned!" Very fortunately, she had a placid temperament and did not get mad. She just laughed. It was such a rude remark; in Japan, it was a most unfavorable thing to have tanned skin.

To make a bath was a tough job, because one had to burn the fuel outside. I was never skilled at making fires. Added to that, it was difficult to cope with the insensitive attitudes of the girls. If they only had made concessions and taken their baths as quickly as they were told, there would have been no problem. But they dilly-dallied under all kinds of pretexts.

One day, it was Sachiko's turn. By then, she was living in the room next to Miss K.. She had become Miss K.'s favorite. I knocked on Sachiko's door and told her that it was her turn to take a bath. But she did not come out. Instead, she gave me an excuse why she could not take a bath now and she would take it later. She knew perfectly well that upsetting the schedule would greatly inconvenience me. I pleaded with her: "Ne, ne, (please, please) take your bath now." She still dilly-dallied. Suddenly, Miss K.'s door burst open. She was equipped with soap and a towel. She said vehemently: "All right. If you make so much fuss, I will take a bath for you." Then she stumped away towards the bathroom.

Miss K., for some reason, did not like me. In hindsight, I realize that maybe someone was telling on me behind my back without my knowledge. I also knew later that she did not have enough wisdom or insight about human nature. She fell for obvious flattery. Perhaps I did not praise her enough to her face. My parents also failed in this department. I overrated her intelligence because, even as a child, I would not have fallen for transparent flattery. It would just embarrass me to listen to such falseness. But I think she liked it. When she burst out of her room, I was surprised. I would rather have thought she would see the reasonableness of taking turns as quickly as possible to make the task easier. I never thought she would rush out with soap and a towel like an angry child.

Washing our clothes and hair was another tedious task. The turn to do so came only once every ten days. While older girls scrambled and grabbed the opportunity, pushing the young ones aside, we young ones made a desperate effort to get our turn. When the turn came on a bath day, we got hot water from the bathtub in a bucket that was used for cleaning the floors. It was also used for washing the material used for our monthly periods. I hesitated to put my head in the water that was in the bucket used for such purposes, but it was the only way we could do it. But it led to a disaster.

One of the girls was a country gentleman's daughter. A country gentleman might have a big house, own big properties and be respected in the area, but his lifestyle was quite different from that in a large city like Tokyo. The middle-class people in Tokyo might live in a smaller house and might not have influence on their neighbors, but their lifestyle was more sophisticated. They were more careful about hygiene and cleaning themselves. This particular gentleman's daughter used to bring back lice after each vacation when she went home.

Now these little insects did not bother her because she was used to them. They normally stayed in the same head as they travelled to Tokyo. But at the time, I was not in the best condition of cleanliness. Trying to cope with group living with my meager thirteen-year-old wisdom and skill, I half looked like a waif. The lice wanted to immigrate to fresh ground and they found it. I had always had an itchy head because I had a lot of dandruff, but all of a sudden, I started having an unbearable itch. I could scratch my head till kingdom come but it would not let up.

One day I became ill and ran a high fever. It was customary for Miss K. to visit sick girls and she came to visit me. I was truly grateful because I knew she did not like me. I raised my head from the pillow and said words of thanks—to her back. After a perfunctory word, she had already turned around to leave. I was very disappointed in her character. She didn't even seem to be able to keep up superficial appearances. This is why I did not convert to Christianity while I was at this school.

The body heat caused by the high fever gave the lice an ideal breeding bed. They must have increased by the hundreds during my illness. Having been cured of my illness, I went back to classes. The itch in my head was driving me crazy. One of my closest friends offered to scratch my head for me. She saw the little creatures running around in my hair. She, out of kindness, did not tell me but went to the class mistress and the information was passed on to Miss K.. At the dinner table she mentioned that we'd better examine our heads because when one was young, one sometimes would get undesirable insects.

My sister looked at my hair and nearly swooned. The operation to attack the lice began. Very fortunately my sister was on good terms with the maid, Toku. She was, at the time, about twenty-eight years old. She was a converted run-away teenager, who had had a wild past life. She had been in an institution, but one day she came in contact with the Christian teaching and it changed her life. How her belief in God changed her was obvious in the photographs she showed us. In one picture she had a dark countenance, full of bitterness and anger. Within two months after Christianity touched her, she looked gentle and content. She was a completely new person.

Toku, because of her wild and lowly past, knew how to get rid of lice. She boiled water, stuck my head in the bowl, wet my hair, poured vinegar onto it and combed it with a fine-toothed comb. She placed the comb at the top of my head and pulled it through my hair with all her might, so that the lice would be scooped up in the comb. Then she quickly immersed it in the hot vinegar water. In between times, she would pick up the eggs of the lice and squeeze them between her fingers. I could hear a "puchi, puchi" sound as the eggs were squashed.

My life at the dormitory was hard and miserable. I was terribly homesick. I missed my family and wanted to get out of this hated communal life. One day, there was a visitor for us. As my sister and I went to the front door, wondering who it could be, there stood a tall handsome young man—our father! Before I could do anything, my sister flew from behind me and hugged him. Perhaps my sister was even more homesick. Now this is the kind of mistake my parents and I made which aggravated Miss K.'s feelings. We did not think of introducing him to her. My father did not think of going to her and thanking her for her care, either. By then, she had made it so clear that she did not like me and I found her attitude childish, I didn't even think of introducing him to her. My sister and I simply got permission from the housemother and went out with our father.

My father had a peculiar talent for finding things other people could not find. So he acquired three tickets to the Takarazuka theatre and "Rakugo" (stand-up comics). Takarazuka was an all-girls theatre school, where they trained young girls to perform. Since it was a school, they had a tough entrance examination. The students performed while they were still at school and after graduation they stayed on to perform. Since it was an all female school, male roles were also played by the girls. Takarazuka was very popular among young girls because, in the days when socializing between a man and a woman was considered to be immoral, Takarazuka girls, who played male roles, were substitutes for satisfying their longing for male companionship. This was why going to Takarazuka theatre was shunned by people like Miss K, because it suggested lesbian relationships.

The night my father took us to Takarazuka, the group "Hana" (Flowers) was performing. The girl who played the male role was Kuniko Ashiwara. She later married a famous artist, who used to paint girls with unique looks, delicate faces with enormous eyes. Kuniko looked so handsome and dazzling that I immediately developed a crush. Beautiful music, the colourful setting and our father with us, I was so happy.

The next day, he took us to the theatre where stand-up comics performed. I did not laugh as much as the grown-ups around me, not because I did not understand the jokes, but I found them not funny enough. My father got worried. He leaned over and whispered: "Aren't you enjoying yourself?" I was enjoying myself and I understood the political innuendo involved in the jokes but my facial muscles did not move. In those days, one had to be extremely careful about what one said on the stage because a Tokko (special police) would be sitting in the theatre and listening. But the entertainers managed to maneuver through the censorial net while at the same time retaining the entertaining quality of their acts. Some of these entertainers were very talented. They could play an accordion and blow a harmonica at the same time. The harmonica was suspended by wires that were tied to their bodies. There were also famous comic duos, who would bounce witty dialogues back and forth like a basketball.

During my unhappy boarding school life, there were a few streams of sunshine. The Christmas party was one of them. There was a dress-up party, where each of us was to dress like a historical or story character and Miss K. was to guess who it was. All the other girls exposed their ignorance and some of them had absolutely no idea what role to play. But I knew at once what to do. I got some soft drapery material and all I needed after that was a basket full of leaves and a piece of cord coiled in it. When it became my turn to give a hint, I simply said: "This is a poisonous snake."

"Cleopatra!" Miss K. was quick to respond. The girls admired her vast knowledge.

Some time before our stay at the dormitory ended, a new girl joined us. She was an American citizen from Seattle, Washington. Like other Japanese-American girls, who had come to Japan to study Japanese, she was a little older than her classmates. She was two years ahead of me. She was one of those people who never ruffled others' feathers. She knew how to cope with life.

The reason she became a boarder was a sad one. While she and her mother were in Japan, the War started and they were cut off from her father who was in the U.S.A. One day when Manabe came home from school, she found her mother dead at the foot of the "karakami" (elaborate sliding door, used only on the inside of the house). The mother's heart gave out from her worries about the War.

As soon as she became a boarder, she became a favorite of Miss K. Since she had an American background, she was socially charming. One day, Miss K. invited Manabe and a few other girls, including my sister and me, to her residence for tea. Unaccustomed to American social graces, we drank tea in silence. Only Manabe was chatting happily and carrying on a conversation with Miss K. Later Miss K. reprimanded us for being silent and not making an effort to make conversation. But in Japan, chatting is considered to be impolite. As one can see from the Japanese tea ceremony, it is a virtue to be silent while one drinks tea.

Manabe had a talent of which I was very envious. She was an excellent pianist. Her future plan was to go to a music conservatory, so she did not just play but she played very well. She could play a lot of tunes by heart.

One evening when we were allowed to have fun, we danced square dances. With the skillful accompaniment played by Manabe, we danced, giggled and forgot our daily woes. In the middle of the active ups and downs, Manabe stopped playing and said: "Let me dance, too!" and tried to join the crowd. But nobody else could play as well as she did, so we mercilessly pushed her down onto the piano stool and the poor thing had to continue to play.

Manabe truly loved music. Whenever I ran into her in the school building, she was playing an imaginary piano while she was walking. I remember how she tilted her head, listening to the soundless music while her fingers were running up and down the scales, which only she could see. I loved listening to her. As soon as she came back from school, she would shut the sliding door that partitioned the dining room and living room where the piano sat, saying charmingly to the girls who were sitting in the dining room: "Excuse me, please. I must play."

She was the opposite of my sister, who was supposed to be practicing the organ. The harmonium sat in the dining room. Very often when I came home, there would be nobody in the dining room and the harmonium sat silently. I used to say to myself: "What a waste! This is the time to play." But my sister had many excuses why she could not practice.

As Manabe played, I hung around and asked her to play Chopin. She tried to please me and played a few passages from Chopin but soon she had to say: "Excuse me, Misao-chan. I must now play examination pieces. Gomenne (forgive me)." Then she would play a Beethoven sonata. I loved that, too and I wished that I could play as well as she did.

All this playing was to prepare for the entrance examination of the music department of Kobe Jogakuin. She did not even attempt to take the examinations of the other conservatories. Being a second generation Japanese-American, she did not have enough knowledge of the Japanese language. She would not have passed any examination given by an ordinary Japanese school. The head of Kobe Jogakuin happened to be a friend of Miss K.'s and was willing to ignore Manabe's lack of knowledge of Japanese and she promised that she would accept her as long as Manabe's piano technique was up to the standard.

So, she travelled to Kobe one day. When she came back, she informed me that she could not answer any of the questions about the history of Japan. So she put down "Nasuno Yoichi" (the famous Japanese samurai-archer who had shot down a fan that had been hoisted up the mast of a boat that had been moving up and down on the waves) for every question. She passed the examination and went on to study music.

Vacations were a problem for my sister and me. Later when I became an adult, I truly understood the problem of our staying at the dormitory during the vacations. The staff would not have any respite, because they had to look after us. Every other girl had a place to go. Some of the girls went home, others went to aunts and uncles, and even the girls from China had some kind of relative to whom they could go. But since our mother was disowned by her family by marrying a Korean, we had no relatives to go to. So we stayed on. This was a rather insensitive thing to do but we couldn't help it.

Toku, the maid looked after us. She, too, had no family, except her baby, so maybe it made no difference to her. She not only cooked us meals, but she also accompanied us to a movie. Miss K. did not approve of close personal contact between the boarders and the maid, so we secretly carried out our outing. I had been learning a lot about different lifestyles since I started living among strangers, but going out with Toku opened up another window.

My father never liked Japanese films. In those days in Japan, it was considered to be a virtue for women not to have opinions of their own. Therefore, the women, in Japanese films, behaved like puppets, spoke hardly any lines and consequently, there was no action in the film. My father preferred foreign films where women spoke up, moved briskly and had a lot of action. My father loved Charlie Chaplin's films. He used to take the whole family to Chaplin's films. I did not quite understand them then, but I am glad now that my father gave me an opportunity to see them. Thus we hardly went to Japanese films. So when Toku wanted to take us to a movie, we did not know that we were going to see a Japanese film.

We went during the New Year's holidays and the theatres were crowded. Toku chose a classical style of film. In a crowded theatre, Toku made use of her experience of having lived among a tough crowd and secured seats for us all. I felt rather awkward surrounded by a kind of crowd that I was not used to. But since it was during the holidays, the film they were showing was entertaining.

On the whole, the old samurai stories were always more interesting than the modern ones. The story revolved around the good and the bad and the plot called for the bad to temporarily have the upper hand to make the story interesting. Toku was completely immersed in the story and called out: "Ey, obnoxious fellow!" or "Oh, go away!" or similar remarks and my sister and I were embarrassed. Toku's baby was peacefully sleeping in her lap while all this was happening.

One day, after Japan had lost one important battle in the South Sea, food almost disappeared from our dining table. Rice had already been rationed and we could not eat as much as we wanted, but we still had something to eat. But one day, we had so little rice that we had to scrape the bottom of the rice container to put some rice in each rice bowl. Sachiko's cheeks pouted out and she said in an irritated voice: "Terrible! We are like children at an orphanage!" Coming from a city in China where there was still food, she did not quite grasp the true situation of the War. It was not the fault of the housemother. Japan was now definitely on the defensive and all the soldiers on Atts Island committed suicide. I am sure that the military had never dreamed of such an event. We started eating watery pumpkins. After this experience, after the War, I never wanted to look at another pumpkin, let alone eat it. I tolerate them only in windows on Halloween nights.

After school when we came back to the dormitory, the housemother had put out plates of snacks on the table. They were very often pieces of sweet potatoes. My eyes, out of hunger, were trained to ascertain which piece was slightly bigger than the others. Even unto this day, I can just glance at pieces of cakes and can tell which one is bigger than the others.

Since we could not get extra food at the dormitory, we went to town in search of anything edible. It was very seldom but sometimes a Japanese tea parlor would sell "oshiruko" (sweet Indian bean soup). With the instinct of a beast on the trail of prey, one of the girls would find out and pass on the information. The school did not approve of our entering such shops, but our hunger was too strong to be obedient to the rule.

The only available food was, though only occasionally, "senbei" (flat round biscuits) made of "kaoliang". Usually these senbei were made of rice flour but since rice flour was not available, it was made of koaliang, a Chinese field product, which was normally given to cattle. It had one drawback. It expanded in the stomach and made one very gassy. It was almost painful when the stomach was full. In order to digest this unhealthy food, we ran up and down the stairs in the house.

In the meantime, my relationship with Miss K. deteriorated even further, like Japan's situation in the War. I never knew the true reason why she so disliked me. I always wanted to ask her but before I did, she died. She went about it like a child, without controlling or hiding her emotions. She did not even seem to have Christian tolerance. Later I thought, maybe it was due to the fact that she was pure Japanese. Despite the fact that she studied in the U.S.A., she did not quite understand the foreign temperament which I possessed. I overrated her intelligence.

My parents had been contemplating removing my sister and me from the dormitory and making other arrangements to keep us in Japan. Nothing was definite yet. But I so wanted to leave the boarding life. However, before I left the dormitory, one final blow came.

One evening, after evening prayer, Miss K., almost trembling with anger, said to me: "Apparently you promised your place here to someone else. Her mother came and told me that. What right have you got to take over yourself the authority to make such an arrangement?" I was stunned. I was also furious. How stupid could she be to believe in such a lie? Was it not common sense that I had no authority to make such an arrangement for someone else? Why was she accusing me of something I had not done? Why did she not even check whether it was true or not? She seemed to have a great character flaw to me.

I shouted: "I never did such a thing!" Tears poured down my cheeks, not because she accused me, but because she was unjustly accusing me of a deed I had never done. Who was this mother who did not hesitate to play a trick at the expense of a child? For years I wanted to find out who this woman was and wanted to ask Miss K., but I never found out. I will find out when I get to the afterlife.

The whole room fell silent. Nobody moved. The rest of the girls were frozen in shocked silence. They were also too surprised to see a girl talk back to an authority like Miss K..

Miss K., who was not expecting a violent protest like mine, got up and stormed out. I kept on crying, mainly because I couldn't forgive the injustice of the accusation, but then, gradually, worry crept into my crying. Whether she was right or not, I was still living under her roof and was a student at her school. She had a right to expel me from my domicile and I would not be able to fend for myself. The housemother, who usually tried to keep to neutral ground and was careful not to get embroiled in any dispute, showed sympathy this time. I think she could sense the childishness of the whole affair. She actually comforted me verbally and patted me while she told me to stop crying.

"Now you'd better go and apologize to her", she said in a kind tone, "Whether she is right or not does not matter. You will have to apologize." She said she would accompany me. She led me to Miss K.'s residence and knocked on the door. "Misao came to apologize to you", she said. I could tell that Miss K. was still fuming.

"Do you really feel sorry? I doubt it," she spat out.

"What do you think?" I said to myself. Why should I feel sorry when I had done nothing wrong? I came to apologize simply because I had no other place to go. I was still sobbing. Miss K. and I did not look at each other at all because our pride was too hurt and we did not truly reconcile with each other. We simply patched up the wound and pretended it was healed. After a few grumbling sounds, she dismissed me but she had not forgiven me and I did not forgive her. I despised her and resolved firmly that I would never become a Protestant Christian.

My sister wrote home about the incident and my mother wrote her back, defending my deed. She did not blame me but said: "Misao must have had her own reasons. It's all right." She just hurried with her plan to find us another place to stay.

chapter XV

My parents found a place to rent, near Tokyo, which was almost a miracle in those days. The house was in Haramachida, in the outskirts of Tokyo. The train, to reach this place from downtown, ran every half an hour. But from Haramachida to our school, it was a straight passage by commuter train. It so happened that the husband of the couple, who were living in this house, found a job in Peking. He was a schoolteacher and wanted to have an adventure by leaving Japan and working abroad. So my parents found them a house to rent in Peking and in exchange, they would let us have the house in Haramachida. The couple moved to Peking with high hopes but was soon disillusioned because a teacher's salary was not sufficient to provide for a life of luxury. The inflation in Peking was very high. Apparently, the wife complained that she had thought she would at least be able to eat Chinese noodles more frequently but couldn't.

My parents came back with my younger sister and we all stayed at a medium class hotel in Shinjuku. To my dismay, I discovered that my mother had been influenced by the women of the Japanese community in Peking. She was wearing a Western style dress and Western shoes. Very unfortunately, she did not have the figure for Western clothes and her behaviour and walk were all wrong. I was embarrassed to be seen with her. So I walked a few steps behind her. My relationship with my younger sister was not very close. Keiko, after having monopolized our parents for one whole year, must have felt uncomfortable in the presence of the two older sisters who suddenly appeared.

My father went back to his job after a few days' stay in Japan. My mother and we, the children, went to the house on the day the previous residents of the house were supposed to move out. This house had only three rooms and a fair-sized bathroom (in the Japanese sense; the bathroom was where the bathtub stood, not the toilet), but there was a yard that had a chicken coup with two hens which produced eggs. When we went to the house, we expected to see it almost empty with only a few items to be removed, as they were to leave for Peking on the same day. When we entered the house, we walked into a sea of clutter, all scattered on the floor. It was almost like two garage sales put together. The wife had a baby on her back and was roaming around aimlessly among the insurmountable mess. I can't remember how much longer it took to put her out of the house, but we finally managed to say "good-bye" to her and had the house all to ourselves; that is, we had the house and much of the clutter to ourselves. My mother as usual took it upon herself to clear and clean up the house. For the next three days, she piled up the junk in the yard and burned it. In a way, it was a pity to burn it all at once, since heating a bath would have required a lot of burnable items, but she could not stand watching it. She swept the yard and polished up the doors and windows. After one week, one of the neighbours dropped by.

"Is this the same house?" he asked.

My mother also visited the neighbours all around, taking a present of apples, a rare commodity in those days, apologizing ahead of time for the noise my sister's organ playing would cause. It is human nature to respond nicely if someone acts nicely first, so everyone assured her that it would be no bother if the sound of the organ came floating out. She also visited the farmers nearby and opened up a black market route so that we would have enough food. We ate more decently than when we were boarding at the school. She even built a bookcase and all the books were neatly lined up.

It was during this period that I started drifting away from my mother. Ever since I was a child, my way of thinking had been Korean and not Japanese. Korean women are frightfully logical. My mother, like many other women, who had only a high school education, was not very philosophical or logical. On top of that, she was pure Japanese. She and I started arguing a lot, she always going off the point of the argument. We were not talking at the same level.

Our arguments used to go like this:
I would say: "I don't think such-such-a-thing is right."
She would say: "Do you speak against your mother?"
Or, I would say: "Please don't talk while I am studying."
She would say: "Do you want me to die?"

I discovered later, though, that even some university graduates did not always stick to the point of the argument. Maybe some women are never logical.

My mother stayed with us for six months and left with Keiko for Peking to rejoin my father. Before she left, she hired a maid for us. She was a daughter of a farmer who lived nearby. Poor Kazue! She was only twenty something and had to look after two teenagers. Previously, she had been working in the household of the president of a university in Tokyo.

The president, unbeknownst to anybody, was Korean. He had a name that could pass for a Japanese name, when read in the Japanese way, so people did not know that he was actually Korean. The family, therefore, was well off and was doing much better than the average Japanese. Poor Kazue, after having seen the president's family and us, got the wrong notion that marrying a Korean would bring her prosperity. I wanted to correct her simplistic way of interpreting life; being Korean means enduring racial prejudices, putting up with the violent Korean temper and many other small differences of a foreign race, but I didn't know how to. I was just amazed by the people who judged things so superficially. She wanted my parents to find her a suitable Korean husband. She also liked the pay my mother offered her. Fifty yen a month was a lot of money in those days. Kazue, being a poor farmer's daughter, had never seen such a large sum of money before.

Looking back I wish I had a little more understanding of life, but wisdom comes only with age. I was only fourteen, fifteen years old. However, I did not treat Kazue as harshly as other Japanese families would have done with their maid, because even as a young girl, I had learned that all human beings were equal. My experience as a Korean had taught me that.

By the summer of 1944, the school had to close down. We were all sent out to work in the factories. Other schools had already closed and the students were working in the munitions factories. Miss K. resisted the order of the military government to follow that example. Even if I didn't like her, I respected her guts. She was summoned everyday by the special police to be questioned as to why she still had the school open and wasting time, while every bit of labour was required to fight the War. She finally had to succumb to the pressure of the military.

My sister's class was sent to a factory where they made parts for airplanes. The girls were supposed to scrape the parts made of "beekrito" to precise measurements. God knows which airplanes could fly with these parts in them. It was obvious that this was a wasteful activity that merely gave the pretence that they were being useful in the War effort. Frankly, it would have been far more useful if they had stayed in school and learned something that would contribute to the future of the country.

Where my sister worked, one day, suddenly, a government inspector appeared and asked: "Are there any foreigners here? Koreans or Taiwanese?" All of a sudden the girls' eyes were fixed on the floor and stony silence filled the room. The inspector left awkwardly after a few minutes. He obviously did not understand why the girls did not answer. He had no idea there could be people who would not discriminate against others because of their different race.

My class was sent to a famous laundry by the name of Hakuyo-sha. Miss K. sent us there because the owner of the company was a Christian and her friend. Before we started the actual work, the manager gave us a talk about the company. It consisted of many interesting anecdotes. Since the company was the biggest and most prestigious, the royal family sent their clothes there to be cleaned. Once, the empress' white fur was sent there to be cleaned. As the workers used a certain chemical, the fur turned green. The faces of the executives also turned green. Spoiling a thing that belonged to the royal family meant severe punishment. The whole company scrambled to find a measure to remedy the apparent damage. Very fortunately, the fur, for no reason, went back to its original colour and saved the executives from punishment.

Our task there was to wash, supposedly, soldiers' uniforms. But there were hardly any soldiers' uniforms because they could not send the uniforms back home to be cleaned. The soldiers were fighting in dirty uniforms and could not take them off, and there was no transportation to send them back if they could even take them off. So after cleaning a few soldiers' uniforms, we were cleaning ordinary citizens' clothes. I was horrified to discover that they were washing British-made suits with water and soap, instead of dry cleaning them. There were no chemicals to use for dry cleaning.

Since there was no fuel, with which to make hot water, we washed everything with cold water. We stood on a wooden board that was placed on the concrete floor, placed an item on a wooden table and scrubbed it with soap and a kind of brush made out of bamboo shreds. Hands became red and raw from the constant use of cold water, and the water that ran constantly on the table and then onto the floor, made the whole body cold. After one week of this hard labour, one was rescued by being moved to another easier job, namely ironing.

We ironed British-made suits, blouses, women's skirts and men's white shirts. A young male apprentice taught us how to iron and fold the shirts properly. One day I came back from lunch and started ironing again. Without checking, I banged down the iron with great vigour onto a man's white shirt. The smell of burning rose from the material. I hurriedly removed the iron. Too late. There was a brown patch on the neck of the shirt. I wailed. Upon hearing my voice, the apprentice came over and nonchalantly said: "Oh, this! This is nothing." He took a silver coin out of his pocket, wet the patch and scrubbed it with the coin. The shirt lost some fibre but we were the only ones who knew about the burn.

One of the other girls was not so lucky. She burned the jacket of a British-made suit, which was not replaceable. One of the regular workers, a middle-aged woman, got on the phone (in those days, the apparatus was on the wall) and called the client. I could hear the annoyed male voice coming out of the phone. The woman was apologizing profusely.

"Yes, sir. We don't know what to say, we don't know what to say. But these girls are inexperienced."

The apology was going on, while the student stood beside her like a sheep about to be sacrificed.

In order to avoid washing clothes and standing on the concrete floor without boots, I called in sick often and took refuge in a movie theatre. Sometimes, I went with friends, but in order to keep it a secret, I often went by myself. There was no guarantee that they might not snitch on me.

One morning, I went to the theatre to see a French film. In order not to be seen and recognized, I went in early and sat in the dark. The film began. Then the door opened and two figures crept in. In the flicker of the light coming from the film, I could clearly see two of my classmates.

One of the silly restrictions the government imposed upon us forbade us to wear anything colourful. We were also forbidden to wear skirts. We were supposed to wear the Japanese traditional peasant trousers, called "monpe", but as usual, I ignored the order and wore my father's trousers. Our hair was supposed to be tied and not to hang loosely. All these restrictions were imposed on top of a hungry stomach.

The women from the "Aikoku Fujinkai" (Society of Patriotic Women) stood at the corner of streets and handed out a sheet of paper upon which it was written "Stop being extravagant. Cut the sleeves of kimonos short." I hated them. They were all middle aged and not pretty. I always suspected that the main reason, why they were so enthusiastic about trivia like this, was that they could not get a man's attention. They must have taken sadistic pleasure in being mean to better-looking women. For that, they had a just cause. Even my classmate's mother was fuming one day. "What does cutting the sleeves short have to do with winning the War?" What was irritating was that the voice of reason was silenced by one barbaric cry of "traitor!"

The company I worked for, managed to procure some rice, and started treating us to a mid-afternoon snack of sloppy rice. At three o'clock, we marched into a room where there were tatami mats. On long tables, they placed big bowls of softly boiled rice. Everyday it gave us a little comfort.

One day, an air-raid alarm sounded. We all stopped working and huddled into an air-raid shelter. But before I went in, I grabbed a book to read. Its title was "Stella Dallas." If the special police had found out about the book, they would not have been pleased. It was an American novel. Suddenly there was a thud and a big male figure came tumbling in. It was the manager who gave us the talk when we first came to work. We, girls, knew that he was a nice man but we lovingly nicknamed him "Cannon" because his nose was rather turned up. We secretly snickered when the "Cannon" joined us in the air-raid shelter during the air raid.

"Mr. Cannon" looked worried. He must, like me, have known that Japan was losing the War and this air raid could be serious. Although the military government had been boasting that the sky over Japan was protected, just one solitary feeble-looking airplane flew over. It flew around like a lost waif, helplessly, in the clear blue of the sky. One of the girls could not contain herself any longer. She wailed: "What are the Japanese soldiers doing? Don't they have any more planes?" No, they didn't. I wanted to tell her but controlled myself. I knew by then that my opinion as a half-Korean girl was not the same as that of the pure Japanese girls. I had heard the other girls whispering: "M.—san is not Japanese. She wants Japan to lose."

I was careful not to voice my opinion. I did not tell them that my gut feeling was that Japan would lose the War within six months and I would need to know English, and that I was secretly preparing for it by studying the language by myself.

At the outbreak of the War, the military government forbade the use of the English language. This caused us a bit of inconvenience because a lot of English words had been adapted in Japanese, e.g. butter, door, ski, skate and a lot more. One could no longer play baseball because all the terms used in the game were American-English. Someone made a feeble attempt to find suitable Japanese equivalents. It was almost comical and awkward with the long Japanese translation. A runner would have collapsed even before he started running. Once, a woman was struck by a chauvinist because she opened a German book while on a commuter train. The fool could not distinguish German from English because they had the same alphabets.

Actually, by then, the government had realized that in order to win the War, one had to understand the enemy, and to do that, one had to know the enemy's language. So the rule against learning English had slackened a bit. Our English teacher, Miss Takahashi, who later became the secretary to the Mrs. Vining, the governess to the Crown Prince of Japan (now the Emperor), was giving us classes in English.

Very fortunately, the alarm did not last long, but even then, I was able to read quite a few pages of "Stella Dallas".

At around this time, my sister and I started noticing three university students riding the same commuter trains in the morning. From the uniforms they wore, we knew that they were students studying at Hosei University. One of them was short, another was of average height and average looks, and the third one was tall and rather handsome. Even the two, who were not so distinguished-looking, had the fresh intelligent air of university students. Just as we noticed them, they noticed us.

Since the trains ran every twenty minutes during rush hour, we were bound to take the same train since we had to reach our destinations at a certain hour. We tacitly waited for each other. One morning, we were a bit late coming and I could see the short one standing outside the station, looking in our direction, agitated. As soon as he saw us, he nodded and darted inside the station. Apparently he was keeping watch and reported our coming to the other two. When the train pulled in, we got on at one door of the car while they got on at another.

In the train, we cast our glances in each other's direction from time to time. We did not even speak to each other, but these meetings were rays of sunshine in the dark drab cloud of the War.

In the summer of 1944, my father came to check on how his two daughters were doing. He stayed a few weeks, but he did not quite grasp the seriousness of the War. He saw us playing hooky, and thought we were skipping classes. We were merely trying to escape from the dreariness of the manual labour. I thought my mind was going numb. At least my father, seeing the lack of food, ventured out into the countryside to acquire food. He was successful and brought back some supplies, which enriched our meagre table. Kazue was pleased and looked happy having a grown-up male in the house.

He also went downtown and bought an electric record player together with records of Verdi's "La Traviata" and Tchaikovsky's "Swan Lake". The stores in the very core of the city were selling off their goods, because they knew that the city would be bombed very soon. Some children were separated from their parents and evacuated to the countryside. Therefore, he got these items at a bargain price. Already, power was cut off for hours during the day, and the needle we used for the record player was no longer made of metal. It was made of bamboo. The ever-so-inventive Japanese created a little gadget that resembled a nail clipper to sharpen the tip of the bamboo needle. The bamboo was so soft that after one use, the tip became blunt. Even if we sharpened the tip, we could see the powder coming off the needle onto the record and we could tell the ridges of the record were spoiled. But I listened. With bamboo powder clouding the surface of the record, I listened. As I was starving for something beautiful, I sat and listened and cursed when the power went out.

One day, my father took us downtown to see a German film. It was a bright summer day. The story was about a young girl who went to stay with her widowed aunt in Berlin. The aunt had been married to an army officer. I remember that, when the niece asked: "Then why did uncle not do this?" or "Why was he not here?", this aunt answered every question with "Official business". They planned to go and see the Berlin Olympics. When they got to the gate, the aunt remembered that she had left the tickets at home. She had to go back home to get them. While the young girl was waiting for her return, a young man invited her to go in with him. From then on, the love story unravelled. But before the film ended, the air-raid siren was sounded. We all had to get out. When we got out, the bright sunshine greeted us. The clear sky looked so far removed from the War; it looked strange. There was no sign of the American bombers. It was a false alarm.

We walked a short distance and my father led us to a Chinese restaurant. It was astounding that any restaurant could still be operating. But this place had food. My father must have gotten to know the owner through a connection in China, because he knew this man's name. The man's name was Chang. He was clad in a sparkling white gown (where did he have it cleaned so beautifully?) and was sitting in the dining room. In the kitchen, a cook was stirring a huge pot with a stick. He was stripped to the waist and his bronze-coloured upper body showed strong muscles. After he glanced at us for a moment, he turned back to his cooking pot and worked at it, completely ignoring us. Mr. Chang looked sagacious with his dark-skinned face that contrasted with the white gown he was wearing. My father asked him: "Mr. Chang, what do you think of the War?"

He stared at my father for a moment as if to ascertain his true intention. Then he almost chanted: "Oh, yes, Japan will win. Japan will win." It sounded to me like: "Oh, yes, Japan will lose, Japan will lose."

Forty-six years later, I finally saw the end of the film I so reluctantly had to abandon in 1944. One of my friends' had a friend, who is of German lineage, and collects German items. His collection also consists of German films. One day I was invited to a dinner at their place, and for the after-dinner entertainment, we were going to watch a German film.

When he asked me what I would like to see, I said: "I don't know the German title, but in Japanese, it was something like 'Concert of Hope'."

"Ah", he said immediately, "Wuensch Konzert". And he played it for me. That's how I saw the ending of the film, finally!

Germany, unlike Japan, continued to produce romantic films, even during the War. Even war films contained, besides propaganda, romances. The women were dressed nicely and there were love stories in the films. We were shocked to see the hero of the "Wuensch Konzert" hang the "Do not disturb" sign on his door so that he could write a love letter in peace.

I don't know how the importer of the film managed it, but once a Viennese film was shown in a theatre in Tokyo. It was a biographical film about the father of numerous beautiful waltzes, Johann Strauss. People, who had been hungry for entertainment, started lining up early in the morning. Two of my classmates and I took turns lining up. As I was lining up, with a book in hand, one of them came over to talk to me. She was not a very nice-looking girl, but I could see that she did her best to dress up. She had on a black sweater and black slacks and a silver locket was hanging around her neck. Lockets were in vogue in 1944. Her black outfit was not suitable for her dark skin. After she had spoken a few words to me, she left to do something else. One of the male university students, who were standing in front of me, said out loud: "What's that? She looks awful." They did not seem to care that I knew her. I cringed and did not know how to look. It was a criticism directed at my friend but I felt insulted myself.

The film was breathtaking. Enchanting Viennese waltzes permeated throughout the film. The rich costumes were dazzling. The women were tall and beautiful. When it ended, we were spat out into the dark dismal grey world of the War. How I longed for peace!

Japan struggled along. All the windows of the houses were covered with dark material so that the enemy planes would not spot us. Shops downtown were closed, all able-bodied men were drafted and we were hungry. In place of healthy men, women and sick men, who were supposed to be at home, nursing their illnesses, were working. On the commuter trains that my sister and I used, we started seeing a young man with throat tuberculosis working as a conductor. His pale cheeks were flushed pink by a fever that did not go away. He had bandages around his neck and coughed a unique consumptive cough.

Despite the dismal surroundings, my friends and I ventured out again, this time to a vocal recital. The shortage of electricity was supplemented by our young energy. Our vibrant circulation of hormones ignited the necessary energy. A famous mezzo-soprano, Fumiko Yotsuya, was to perform in a hall downtown. I can't remember how we managed to get the tickets but we went. Very fortunately there was neither an air-raid nor an outage of power to interrupt the performance. I can't remember how full the hall was. All I remember was that Miss Yotsuya sang "Connais-tu le Pays", an aria from the opera "Mignon" by A. Thomas, in Japanese. On the way home, we giggled in the streetcar, imitating her and the man standing next to us became amused and started laughing. I sent him a sideways glance and acted coyly.

In February, 1945, I was walking downtown on the street near the Hibiya movie theatre. The Hibiya theatre was one of the theatres that played mainly foreign films. I had my hair hanging down to my shoulders, a colourful ribbon around my head with a bow on the top and a jacket with multi-coloured-stripes, which my mother sent me. (She had no idea that the Japanese government did not approve of colourful outfits because she was in Peking, China). The way I was dressed was in the utmost defiance of the Japanese ordinance. If a Kenpei (special police) officer had happened to be around, he would have arrested me and put me on a truck, to send me to work in a dark coal mine pit in Hokkaido. Fortunately, the Kenpei were also suffering from the shortage of staff and could not send men out to check on unpatriotic traitors in colourful jackets.

I looked at the theatre and it was announcing that a German film would be shown in three minutes. In those days, the theatres were not sure when power would be available, so they started showing films whenever there was power. Obviously, the Hibiya theatre had power at that moment. I paid the admission and went in. The theatre worker did not question why I, in a multicoloured jacket, was not working. Inside, in the dark, I counted about ten people of like soul. The film started rolling, as if in defiance of the War.

The title of the film was "Die Heimat" (Home). It was about the Germans who lived in Poland and were forced to repatriate because Germany was losing the War (they did not say it but put it in such a way that the Poles were persecuting them.) One beautiful woman, who took the lead, comforted her fellow countrymen and led them back safely to their Homeland. There was a scene, when they were put in prison, in which this woman sang. The beauty of her voice enthralled me. It was a film full of propaganda but just seeing a foreign film was enough to give me joy. I got home safely without getting caught.

chapter XVI

March 1945 arrived.

My parents wanted us to leave Japan and join them in Peking. I was so thrilled with the idea that I went around telling everyone that I would leave school before the end of March, which was the end of the school year and the end of my school life at Keisen. The information my big mouth was spreading reached Miss K.'s ear. Miss Sasaki, who had known us from the corner house and had been protecting me here and there, called me to her to warn me that I should not be so outspoken. Apparently, Miss K. was outraged and said that if I was going to leave school before graduation day, she would not give me my graduation diploma. I was not really worried about the diploma because for one and half years of that schooling, we were washing clothes and not learning anything. The diploma would have just been a piece of paper and was not representative of what was in my head. But I shut up. I was surprised to see how many complications I could cause. Eventually, I did get my diploma sent to me in Peking. I lost it in the shuffle of the evacuation. My sister never got hers. Hers was lost in the mail.

God works in funny ways. Since both my sister and I had to go to Peking, He made it so that both of us would graduate at the same time. Japan had such a shortage of manpower, the government cut one year off from the required time to graduate from a lycée, so that sixteen-year-olds and seventeen-year-olds could go to work. My sister graduated from her fifth year of joggakko, which was the regular year, but I graduated from my fourth year at the school.

Japan was approaching the final stage of the War. Just before my father came to get us, the Americans started bombing the city of Tokyo. One day, I got on the train to go home and there was a group of people with scorched overcoats, a washbasin and a bundle of goods. One of them was barefoot. In March the weather was still cold, so his feet were red, but he did not seem to feel too much pain because his senses were still numbed from the horrible experiences of the night before. The night before they had been burned out and they were telling the passengers about their experiences in loud voices. Since I had known all along that the Japanese way of defending themselves, with bamboo sticks and a relay of buckets of water, would not work against Americans who had abundant resources, I beheld them with rather cool eyes. I had no empathy for the ignorance of the Japanese. I had nothing but contempt for this War.

Towards the end of March, my father came to get us. We had to leave everything: futons, kitchen utensils, a bathtub and an elaborate American-made harmonium. When the War started, the American missionaries in Peking, who owned this organ, had to leave it behind. They sold it to my mother for 750 Yen, an enormous amount of money in those days. Then she managed to ship it to the organ tuner in Aoyama, Tokyo. It actually did arrive. The organ tuner let us know that it had arrived so my sister and I went to look.

When we saw what was supposed to be a harmonium squashed between two boards of wood, our eyes nearly popped out. The organ tuner, sensing our sentiments, had a peculiar half smile on his face. Soon after that, my mother's letter of enquiry arrived. She then gave orders to restore it as much as possible. The Japanese are incredibly deft people. The organ tuner managed to rebuild it into the shape of a harmonium. Very unfortunately, some of the parts had sunk into the Strait of Korea and were never recovered, so the sound was not exactly what it should have been.

After three days of cleaning up, my father moved us to the Imperial Hotel. Now the Imperial Hotel was situated right in the center of the city. As the Americans were bombing the city according to the "Carpet Bombing" procedure, which meant that they bombed one section, and the next time, they bombed the section next to it, this hotel would be a target in the near future. My father obviously did not have any idea about the bombing, so we stayed at the hotel for three days. For some peculiar reason, the bombing stopped while we were at the hotel.

The luxurious hotel, that used to be filled with bright lights and vivid laughter, was grey and dismal. But the bedding was still clean and the chambermaid came to make our beds. My father gave some oranges to the young chambermaid and she nearly jumped with joy. She said repeatedly: "Thank you", "Thank you." In the morning we were served watery oatmeal. Under the gorgeous chandelier in the dining room, we swallowed the poor breakfast in silence. There was one foreigner, presumably a white Russian, at another table, who was eating his breakfast alone. I wanted to know what this lone foreigner was thinking.

On the day of our departure, we got up at 5:00 a.m. to line up for the train that would leave Tokyo station at 8:00 a.m.. The sky was cold and grey. On the platform, there was already a long queue. We lined up at the tail end of the queue. Behind us, there were only a few other people.

Just before the train pulled in, an army officer arrived with his wife. He glanced at the line and without saying a word, pushed his wife into the middle of the line, a little ahead of us. We all wanted to scream at him, but we did not dare speak against an army officer with a sabre hanging at his side. His wife turned her face away from us pretending not to notice our sentiments. We cast our eyes to the ground, cursing them inwardly. He glared at us as if to say: "Any objection? I am fighting for the country." The train pulled in and people started boarding. But the last person, who managed to get on, was about the fifth person ahead of us. The officer's wife got on so her husband left. My family was left standing on the platform.

But again, God worked a miracle for us. Soon there was an announcement that there would be another train in about ten minutes. Hearing this news, passengers started to rush over to the platform. The platform was soon crowded. But since the previous line ended at about the fifth person ahead of us, we were at the head of the line this time. Soon another train pulled in. Not only did we get on, but we were also able to get seats. In a few minutes, the train was overflowing. Every seat was occupied and people sat in the aisles and in the toilets. I remember two high ranking naval officers had had their secretaries reserve seats near the door. They came in late, without queuing up, and sat there looking comfortable.

When our train arrived in Hiroshima, we discovered why God did not let us ride in the previous train. The train that had left before us, for some peculiar reason, had stopped in Hiroshima and would not go any farther. This meant that the officer's wife was stranded there, this time without the power of her husband's sabre. The passengers, who were forced to get off the train, were madly rushing up and down the platform. Someone banged on the window. He asked in a desperate voice: "Is there any room there for us, please?" Everyone on our train shook our head weakly. We wanted to help them but there was simply no room. We, who were already on, could hardly move our bodies.

We sat in stolid silence until we got to Shimonoseki. We had to spend a night in a dingy inn. Since there was a shortage of cleaning materials as well as other things, the room was not particularly clean and we had to share the room with two other women. I could sense that one of the women immediately showed an interest in my father. I slowly crept under the bedding. The edge of the cover was hard with the cake of dried up human breath, as the inn was not able to clean the bedding for many months, perhaps even years. My skin cringed but there were no other materials for sleeping. I could see from under the cover that the woman was sending glances of a sexual nature toward my father.

The next morning, we went to the pier to line up for the ferry. We were standing in the Japanese line. A stocky middle-aged Japanese "Kenpei" (special police) came to inspect us. It was rare to see a "Kenpei" walking around in those days because all able-bodied men were drafted and the number of "Kenpei" was reduced to a minimum. But since Shimonoseki was the gateway to Korea, they must have assigned someone to catch any undesirable elements. He glanced at my father and his eyes hardened.

"Oi (Hey), aren't you Korean?" he said arrogantly.

"Yes."

"Then, why are you standing here? This is the line for the Japanese. Chosenjin wa achidda. (Koreans are over there)."

My father obviously wanted to protest but did not say anything. He silently picked up his suitcase. So my sister and I did likewise and started to follow him.

He shouted again: "Oi, why are you two following him?"

Despising him, I looked at him and pouted: "BECAUSE he is our father."

His attitude immediately softened. "In that case, you may stay here." We went back to the line and set the suitcases down again. I sneered at him inwardly and laughed at his ignorance of not knowing that Japan would be losing the War—soon. The line moved forward with us Koreans at the tail.

After the ferry docked in Pusan, there were a few hours of waiting before the train for Peking left. We went into the city in search of food. At the corner of a street, a Korean man was standing idly with a look of defiance and a certain amusement. The Koreans, sensing Japan's inevitable defeat, were not afraid of the Japanese any longer. My father spoke to him in Korean: "Have you got anything to eat?"

The man's face disarmed into a grin. "Are you Korean?"

"Yes."

"Your daughters don't look Korean."

"But they are."

"In that case, we can give you something to eat." He led us into a lane and to a house. He opened the front door. He invited us to take off our shoes and come in. We went into a room and sat down. Here was a good traditional Korean family. It consisted of grandparents, parents and children, and the whole house was active from sheer existence of so many human bodies. The man, the head of the family, shouted commands to the womenfolk.

"Cook some rice."

The women in charge went off to the kitchen to carry out the order. The grandmother was spared of labour because of her seniority. So she sat close to us observing. She said to my father: "Are these your daughters?"

"Yes."

"They don't look Korean." Then she called out to the other women. Obviously she said: "Come and see. They don't look Korean." About three women abandoned their duties in the kitchen and came over to look at us. "True, they don't look Korean", they chorused unanimously.

With our stomachs fortified with food, we got on the train. It was crowded as usual and at night, the lights in the train were dimmed. As the train got closer to Peking, it became less crowded and there was enough space to sit comfortably. Across from me, a Chinese woman was sitting. Coming from grey dismal Japan, she looked to me to be the prettiest creature I had ever seen. First of all, she was clad in a velvet dress and her face was made up. Her skin looked as smooth as silk and her lips were red. Her black eyes shone with electric light—mysterious and exotic. I stared at her in admiration for so long that she must have felt uneasy. She turned her face to hide her embarrassment. The train swayed while we slumbered. The next day, in broad daylight, we arrived in Peking and home.

Funnily enough, the city did not strike me as strange. Aside from the fact that it was my second visit, I had grown older and my appreciation of things and my judgment was more mature. I was happy to be in Peking. But I did not quite feel the same about my parents and my younger sister, Keiko. After a few years' separation, my younger sister, Keiko was a stranger to us and my mother was a partial stranger. We had now grown apart in different directions. But her instinctive love for us was still alive

She was aghast to see us so fat. Actually, we were not fat but bloated. Years of starvation and of eating only starchy foods (if available), made us bloat up and tinged our skin greenish. My mother forbade us to go out for about a week and set about reducing us to normal size. She gave us three square meals with a lot of variety. Within a week, we were back to normal and pretty again.

The house, in which we lived, was in an area where the Japanese were living. It belonged to a lady who was half Japanese and half Chinese and married to a Chinese man. She spoke both Chinese and Japanese beautifully. She looked obviously partly Chinese and had a bad case of buckteeth. But she refused to straighten or pull out her teeth and replace them with a denture, because she was afraid that it would affect the pronunciation of her Chinese, which I think would have been true. Teeth have a lot to do with the pronunciation of a foreign language.

Next door to us lived a very nice Japanese family, called Takeda. The husband was in the army but was still coming home from time to time. Their oldest daughter was a nurse, the second daughter was about the same age as my younger sister, and the youngest child was a boy of about four or five. I don't know why they were friendly with Koreans. Maybe they wanted to practise the slogan of "All Asia is one and the same."

Well, it isn't. The Takedas were true patriots. They sincerely believed that Japan was fighting for a just cause. They loved the emperor and were trying to assist the country to bring about victory by doing their share. Little did they know about the rebellious spirit that was boiling in me. It is the blood and the blood is thicker than water.

The Takedas and my family each had a ladder propped up against the tall wall that separated the two houses, and we would climb the ladder whenever we wanted to pass on gossip or information. I appreciated the neighbours and I was happy for my mother. Only, I did not, and could not, share their enthusiasm for the War. I was not Japanese.

One day, their little boy came over to our house and stood in the yard and waved his arms, imitating an airplane.

"Bru-u-n, Bru-u-un, I am going to be a Tokko (Kamikaze suicide fighter) and beat the enemy."

"Isn't he brave?" my mother said in a flattering manner.

"Quatch!" I said after the boy left. "Of course, he would say that. He is too young to be afraid of death!"

My mother was then shocked by the new opinion I expressed: "Japan will lose the War very soon." She was too stunned to accept my opinion. She, like all the other housewives, had never formed any opinion of her own when it came to politics, the world situation or the economy or any other serious subject. Because of the lack of training of her intellect, she was at times quite unreasonable.

"Don't tell me something so awful," she retorted violently. She did not understand that her daughters were half foreigners and mixed races had no definite patriotic feelings for any particular country. She obviously did not know why Japan was fighting, or what against or where it was heading.

In front of our house lived a family by the name of Suzuki. The neighbours, sniffing out the fact like a hound dog, knew that the wife was Korean. She was born Korean but by marrying a Japanese fellow, she became Japanese. My mother, who was born Japanese, became Korean because she married a Korean. The Suzukis were a childless couple. A few months after my sister and I arrived in Peking, suddenly a baby appeared in the Suzuki household.

One day, Mrs. Suzuki came out of the gate, proudly holding a baby bundled up in baby clothes. I looked at the baby and I knew what Mrs. Suzuki did not know. On the right side of our house lived an extended Chinese family. The grandmother of the family came out of the gate to have a look at the baby. When she looked at it, her eyes lit up with malicious pleasure. After Mrs. Suzuki disappeared into the house with the baby, the grandmother faced me with a meaningful smile and said in Chinese: "That baby looks just like the husband." "Yes, it does", I replied and we exchanged smiles that spoke a thousand words.

This was a trick a husband would play if he was married and had a mistress, about whose existence he did not want the wife to know. If the mistress became pregnant and the husband desperately wanted to recognize the child legally without disturbing the peace at home, he would talk his wife into adopting a child. In cases like the Suzukis, it was easy. The wife felt guilty for not being able to conceive a child. So one day, the husband suggested to the wife: "Why not we adopt a child? I know someone who is willing to give up a child. It is healthy and seems to be a nice child." Of course the wife consented. So the child was adopted, became his child legally and the peace at home was maintained.

Next to the Suzukis, lived another Japanese couple. The husband was quite a bit older than the wife. It was rather doubtful that they were legally married. I guessed that the young wife used to be in an occupation which housewives despised. The husband was shy and seemed to be the kind of person who would worry about what other people would say about his relationship with this young woman. I also sensed that this young woman was the best thing that had happened in his dull life. When I saw him, he would bow deeply several times. Every time he bowed, his long side hair (it was long on the sides to hide the bald spot at the top) would dangle down and he would clumsily scoop it up with his hand. His young wife may not have had class but she seemed to be a good-natured woman. But this couple was the topic of conversation of the Chinese yancho men (rickshaw men) who loitered in the street, waiting to be hired.

One day, the houseboy of the couple appeared at the gate and shouted to summon a yancho. "Mrs. So-and-so is going to a doctor. Her _____ is sick!" The yancho men burst out laughing. The Chinese took revenge on the Japanese in various subtle ways. When the wife came out without knowing what had happened, the yancho men's laughter had subsided but their eyes were shining with their dirty imaginations and vulgar sneers.

On the corner of the street lived the Okadas. Mr. Okada had some high position in a company. Mrs. Okada was trying to act as though she came from an upper-class family, but everyone knew that her background was not what she pretended it to be. She was a walking example of the "petit bourgeois". The amah, who was still working for my mother, told us that a few days after our arrival, Mrs. Okada asked her: "Are those girls beautiful?" because Mrs. Okada prided herself on her being the best looking woman in the city. In fact, she was just an ordinary-looking housewife. The amah, who also did not think much of her looks, answered with exaggerated enthusiasm: "Yes, they are great beauties!" By the time this conversation had taken place, my mother had succeeded in restoring our usual looks.

Mrs. Takeda, very kindly, made me a summer dress out of blue cotton kimono material. She said it would look better on me than on her own daughter. Indeed it looked very nice on me and I was delighted to have a new dress after the years of austerity in Japan. Only I felt very bad that I could not reciprocate their love for Japan with the same enthusiasm.

One day, I came home from an outing in this dress. The yancho men were idling and obviously gossiping in the street. When they saw me, one of them got up and walked towards me. Apparently, the rest of the group sent him to me as the envoy because he could speak Japanese.

"You know", he said, "we, Chinese, have beautiful women, too. It isn't that we don't have them. But we have concluded that at the moment, you are the most beautiful girl in the whole of Peking."

chapter XVII

Life in Peking was wonderful. I was out of school and no longer had to follow the orders of my superiors. There were no examinations to write and there was no more working in a laundry. A few days after we arrived in Peking, spring rushed into the city with a sandy storm. The weather suddenly became warm and it was beautiful. The air was pregnant with the hopes and passions of youth. The spring wind was so sandy, that some of the girls covered their faces with sheer scarves, in order to avoid getting the sand in their eyes. I followed their example. I felt like a mysterious woman from a harem.

The reality of the War had not disappeared. But since China WAS a foreign country, the Japanese war cries were indirect and somehow distant. The only worry we had was what would happen to us when Japan actually lost the War. But it had not happened yet. Although there was high inflation, goods were still in the shops and all one needed was money. The only thing one could not get was sewing notions. There wasn't a yard of ribbon in the whole city. So, young girls used pieces of knitting yarn to decorate their hair. Of course, we followed this example.

A week after our arrival, my father's Korean friends wanted to invite us to a homecoming party at a Chinese restaurant. My sister and I experienced, for the first time, a real Chinese banquet. Koreans are great eaters and they are quite generous about spending their money. So the banquet consisted of seven courses.

My elder sister and I were unused to Chinese dinners, so we tried to eat a lot of the first course. The Korean friend warned us that we should not stuff ourselves with the first course; there would be a lot more to come. True, dishes came one after another, and by the time the dessert came, we were so stuffed, we could not even move. When I heard the dessert was going to be rice dumplings coated with syrup, I thought I would explode. I still remember the red tail of the lobster standing in the middle of a large dish as if to symbolize our departure from constant hunger and arrival at abundant life.

There were two Korean couples at the banquet. One of the husbands, his name was Iwamoto, was working for the Japanese military. He had a sad past. His whole family was killed by Chinese when they were living in Manchuria. The Japanese saw a wonderful opportunity in this poor orphaned Korean boy. They wanted to use him to their advantage. They indoctrinated in him hatred of the Chinese and pounded in him a feeling of revenge. They taught him over and over again that the Chinese were his enemy and the poor boy was brainwashed. He had no qualms about working for the Japanese against the Chinese. He was a nice frank young man. My heart ached for him and I hated the Japanese for twisting and poisoning his innocent heart. He respected my father. Maybe he saw in him the idealized image of his deceased father. His wife was a typical Korean woman—very frank, open and outspoken.

The couple was desperately trying to have children. At the German hospital in Peking, the wife even underwent the drastic surgery of having her internal organs taken out, massaged and put back in her body—three times. One doctor told her that she had cooled her body too much. As she had lived in Manchuria, where the temperature could go down to 40 degrees below zero, she happily went skating with in very little clothing. She was ever so sorry that she did not protect her organs against the severe winters of the Continent.

One week later, the other couple, who was also at the banquet, invited us to another Chinese restaurant. There, again, we enjoyed a similar banquet. The wife of this couple looked so pretty to us. Her white skin was so smooth, her eyebrows were so dark and her lips were shiny red. She looked so beautiful to me that I could not take my eyes off her. A few days after the banquet, my elder sister and I were walking down the street and a woman passed by us on a yancho. When she saw us, she leaned over from the yancho and bowed to us, smiling. We returned bows but could not recognize her. We went about ten yards, saying to each other: "Who is she?" Then it dawned on us that she was the wife of the second couple without make-up. We burst out laughing. I made up my mind then that I would like to have the kind of looks that would look nice even without make-up. I think now, though, make-up is a good thing. A woman must have it.

The Chinese defied the Japanese authorities and led their lives in the way they saw fit. They knew that Japan was losing the War but hid the knowledge with eerie silence. One fine day, a young man in a nice suit (in those days, the Japanese no longer wore suits; they wore Mao suits. The Mao suit was not the invention of the Chinese. They took over the outfit the Japanese were wearing in 1945) and a tall young woman in a pink traditional Chinese costume strolled down the main street of Wan Fu Ching, arm in arm. It looked like a demonstration of defiance against the Japanese rule. They took their time walking down the street and when they reached the end of the street, they turned around and came back at a slow pace. People, Chinese and Japanese alike, stopped to stare at them. In China, no decent woman, young or old, would have been seen outside of her home, in pink. Bright colours would only invite trouble. So the pink dress on this young woman stuck out like a crane's neck among ducks.

After long years of not having pretty dresses, my elder sister and I were consumed with the desire for new clothes. My poor father managed to squeeze out some extra money to buy us jackets. We went to a fabric shop to have them made. One of the salesmen had pale skin, unique to a lot of Chinese, and was rather unfriendly. Obviously, he did not like the Japanese. Another salesman, a short Cantonese-looking man-, was friendly. He had dark skin and was very charming. When it came to measuring us he said: "Your elder daughter is plump. She will need more material." My poor sister, for no reason, started putting on weight while we were in the dormitory and she was very unhappy about it. But unlike diet-conscious North Americans, she did not go on a diet to reduce her weight. We knew that it was not the result of eating.

Since both my sister and I had been starved for years, we would never voluntarily go on a diet or cut down on food. So my sister stayed plump for several years, until suddenly one day, she slimmed down again without taking any measures. The charming Cantonese man jumped around us, trying to please us. The measurements were taken and the fabric was chosen. Some days later, we went to get the jackets. Together with the jackets, I came out with a crush on the dark-skinned salesman.

We wore the pink jackets proudly, without fear of getting caught by the secret police. There were no more drills. We did not have to darken the rooms at night. The movie theatre was showing foreign films day and night. My sister and I went to such films often and sometimes the whole family went together. Before the showing of the film, they announced regularly that we should look under our seat to check whether or not there was a bomb. This was the only reminder that we were still in the War.

One day, I can't remember why, I went to the theatre alone at ten o'clock in the morning. It was cool inside the theatre and there were only a few people sitting in the dark. When the announcement came, I did not even bother to look. Somehow I never felt anything that had to do with this War would hurt me. I just admired the ability of the Chinese, who could learn Japanese well enough to make the announcement, because the Japanese were notorious for inability to learn foreign languages. There were many Japanese who had been in China for thirty years and could not speak more than two words in Chinese.

At around this time, my sister and I became keenly conscious of our Korean blood. We discovered that our indifference and dislike of the War did not stem only from the lack of materials and the inconvenience caused by it. We couldn't care less about this War because we were not pure Japanese and had no patriotic feelings for Japan. We were NOT Japanese. While we were still at school, the emperor's edict on the War was read out on the date of the Declaration of the War, which happened to be 8th of each month. When everyone's head was bowed deeply in reverence, I wanted to laugh. To my surprise, my sister had the same sentiment. So far, my being half Korean just taught me about racial prejudice. Suddenly being half Korean took on a different meaning. It was the blood that counted. My sister and I came to the realization that since we were mixed, we would never be able to totally understand the Japanese- nor love Japan unconditionally.

While we were walking around in our pink jackets, skirts and dresses, the Japanese were still wearing "monpe"(peasant trousers). One bright day, at the corner of the street near Ton Tang Pai Row, a group of Japanese women were standing in a cluster. They were wearing "monpe" in dark colours. They looked strange and out of place, since the Chinese looked completely unconcerned about the War and it was obvious already that Japan would not win the War, whether they wore "monpe" or strapless evening gowns. The group of women looked pathetic and almost comical.

We soon learned, however, that the Japanese were still serious about the War. One day, Mrs. Takeda, our kind neighbour, appeared at our communication station at the top of the wall and whispered to us: "If you are not working, go and find a job quickly. Mrs. Okada asked me 'Are those girls working? If not, I will go to the Kenpei (special section of the police) and tell on them!'" I groaned.

Don't these Japanese know that they are losing the War and it's just a matter of time? It's useless to work for the cause. In fact, all the graduates of the girls' school, where my sister and I attended for only three days before we quit, were sent to the hospital in Peking and were working there. They were not even allowed to go out and were virtual prisoners. It made us shudder to think that we could have been confined to the hospital with the Japanese and been forced to work for the cause we did not believe in. The French films with Jean Gabin and Daliell Dalieux would have been out of reach.

My father immediately went to his Japanese superior, who was sympathetic towards my father. We definitely did not want to work in a hospital or any other place that was connected with the War. If we did, the minute the War ended, the Chinese would come and take us prisoners. What we wanted was nominal work, a pretence, so that we could prove that we were working.

The superior introduced us to a small office that was headed by a dandy attractive man. He was spared from the draft because he had an advanced case of consumption. He had been to Europe and hated the

War. Surprisingly, the staff included three more able-bodied men besides him. There was only one young girl who was doing some clerical work. She seemed to have a much more frank character than other Japanese girls.

The office was situated in the Russian section of the former extraterritorial area. The whole setting of this area had a Caucasian influence, so that it looked like Europe and was very beautiful. The office building was a former Russian house. The doors had handles instead of doorknobs and the toilet was a flush toilet. (The toilet in our house was also a flush toilet.) The house had a fair-sized, well-tended garden with tall trees. My imagination ran immediately to André Gide's novels. I fancied myself as the young French girl who had a crush on an older man. She climbs up one of those trees and waits for the man to come by. He comes. He looks up and asks her why she is up in a tree. She doesn't want him to know that she adores him so she sulks instead and cries inside. I was the heroine because I soon had a crush on the man in charge of the office.

Mr. O took us around and introduced us to his colleagues. He was pleased to add two pretty young girls to his office. He was thin and his cheeks were flushed because of his illness, but he was very attractive and worldly wise. We were hired because he didn't take the War seriously, either. He knew that we just needed the pretence of work.

As soon as we started working, my elder sister, who had more common sense than I, proved to be very useful to the treasurer; whereas, I proved my incompetence immediately. While my sister was assisting the treasurer, I was exposing my inabilities. I claimed to be able to use the abacus, but when I was asked to do some additions, all the answers were wrong. The treasurer, Mr. Ishii was very cross. He pointed out to me my mistakes in a rough voice.

In all of my lifetime, I have never been efficient at work that required my presence from 9:00 a.m. to 5:00 p.m. or for getting along well with colleagues in this kind of environment. I have to have flexible hours and a sporadic amount of work. I soon started to hate going to the office. Added to that, the youngest male staff member began to treat us meanly because we turned down his invitation to go out. Dealing with males, whom we did not fancy, was also a reason why we did not like working in the office.

One day in May, my father came home with the news that Germany had surrendered. By then the Japanese newspaper in Peking had shrunk to one quarter of its regular size and this small newspaper reported Germany's surrender. Italy had already surrendered some time before and now Japan was left alone to keep on fighting. Very little, almost none, of what happened to Hitler was known at the time. The Chinese were listening to short wave radio broadcasts and knew a lot more about the War than the Japanese. They did not change their expressions on the surface, but what was inside them was the calm before the storm.

Despite the calamities in Europe, the Japanese life in Peking went on as usual.

One beautiful summer day, our office had a picnic. The wife of the manager prepared lunch. Before we left for Pei Hai Park, we dropped by Mr. O's house. The family lived in one of the Russian houses near the office. It was also a beautiful house and I envied them for being able to live in such a snazzy European-style house. The wife had laid out the ham, sausages and bread on a tray and was still busily working to get everything ready. When I looked at the tray, I admired her skills of cooking and preparing food. The whole thing looked so professional and elegant. It was quite obvious that she had taken some lessons in Western cooking. I realized anew that I was totally unprepared to be a housewife.

The wife of the manager, contrary to her dandy husband, looked quite plain. It must have been one of those marriages, in which the husband lives a carefree life (including seeing other women) while the faithful wife obediently keeps the house without complaining.

While we were at the park and had opened our lunch package, another Japanese company was having a picnic in the same area. Three young women from that company descended upon us noisily chatting, like an avalanche in spring. Each of them wore a coolie hat with colourful pictures painted on it (it was the fashion) and a cotton summer dress. They didn't look to me to be particularly cultured. I was too young and inexperienced in life and I was in awe of these women, who had abundant worldly knowledge. They did not seem to pay much respect or attention to the manager's wife. They freely picked at and consumed the foods she had prepared so diligently but did not show any appreciation for her efforts. They almost completely ignored her. I sympathized with the manager's wife and confirmed my determination to never marry young and turn into a mere housewife.

Mr. O obviously had many affairs. One day, a middle-aged woman turned up at our office. She was an average-sized Japanese woman, but was clad in Western clothes. Her skin was rather brown (which in Japan was considered to be a defect), and did not look like an ordinary housewife but looked like a working woman. She looked and behaved as though she had no fear about life, because she had been tossed around so much in life that her skin was toughened. She placed herself in one of the chairs despite the fact we were working. Although I was supposed to be working, I was too curious about her so I stopped doing whatever I had been doing and gazed at her with my mouth open.

Someone brought her tea. Her total lack of the usual Japanese modesty fascinated me. She was rattling away about various subjects, all the while insinuating that she and the manager spent time at a resort in China. What she was hinting at was they had an affair and I was wondering why she did not want to hide the fact, but rather was trying to make it public. Later I learned that some women are mean-spirited and want to annoy the wife on purpose, because they are jealous of the happiness of a married woman. She wanted to hurt another woman on purpose because another woman had what she longed to have but could not.

Mr. O came in and greeted her. I wasn't sure whether he was embarrassed by her being there or if they had planned the meeting. He must have invited her to come and visit him in Peking, because they eventually disappeared together, leaving us in awkward silence.

A few days later, I went for a walk in the extraterritorial area and passed by Mr. O's house. I thought I might drop in and say hello. I stopped short of knocking on the door. A heated argument was going on inside the house. A window was open. They had no time to notice my standing right by the window. The wife of the manager screamed: "That woman........" Then I heard the manager shout back, defending his male ego and pride.

The exchange of harsh words went on. After a few minutes, I retreated quietly. I never wanted to get married.

In the area where we worked, there was a big branch office of Yokohama Bank of Species. It employed a large number of Chinese who had learned enough Japanese to work for the bank. During our lunch hour, we went out to the green belt, which lay between our office and the bank. The bank employees came out and played volleyball during the break. Among them, was a rather handsome young Chinese man who wore a traditional "chong—san" (long tunic) and trousers. In fact, I never saw him in Western shirts and trousers, even though a lot of the others wore an open shirt and trousers. He had pale skin and big eyes. When I saw him, I knew he was the one I liked. He looked at me and we knew.

Those summer days were beautiful with clear skies, bright sunshine, tall trees and cool shade. I sat in the shade, while I watched the Chinese employees come out. He came out. Several of the bank employees formed a circle with a volleyball. He, quietly and subtly glanced in my direction. I just looked at him for a fleeting moment. "Yes, I am watching you," the message was conveyed. He turned to his colleagues and played. I could see the hem of his "chong—san" dance as he jumped to catch or toss the ball.

When my office sent me to the bank, the employees noticed me. "There she is!" they were obviously saying to him. Once, the teller who was at the till, got up and vacated the seat and about three employees pushed him from behind so that he could look after me. He was pushed forward, blushing. His Japanese was not as fluent as some of the other employees. He asked me in a voice almost in a whisper: "May I help you?" After he had piled up the bills for me to take (because of the inflation, one had to carry around a large sum of cash), we bowed to each other and I left.

After the end of the War, the romance ended because the employees of the bank were worried about their future and the Japanese were no longer the conquerors. We all had to think of more serious matters but the memory remains like the pink petal of a cherry blossom that is pressed and preserved.

I hated working in an office. But soon, one good thing happened—

I got sick. My lung problem recurred. It brought me a wonderful bonus. I had to quit working. After about two months of working, I had to rest at home. My elder sister would have been happy to have been in the same situation, but she remained healthy, so she grudgingly had to go to the office everyday. According to the general belief of the day, if tuberculous adenitis of the hilum recurred at around the age of seventeen or eighteen, one was sure to be at the gateway of death. But my instinct told me that I would be all right. I never worried.

My mother took me to the Japanese hospital. There were no Japanese doctors left. All medical staff had been drafted and sent to the front to tend the wounded soldiers. A Manchurian doctor saw us. As Manchurians often are, he was dark-skinned, dauntless and handsome.

"Madam", he said to my mother, "there is no medicine left in this hospital."

"What do you have left?" asked my mother.

"Two ampoules of calcium and six ampoules of vitamin B."

"In that case, just inject them all."

He dutifully did so and this was the end of my treatment at the hospital.

Instead of getting medical treatment, I read a book entitled "How to Cure Tuberculosis — Yes, You Can Be Cured." In those days, all the methods recommended were natural because there was no particular medicine to cure it; I think the natural methods are the best anyway. Using strong drugs is far more detrimental to the body than the illness itself. I faithfully practised the methods recommended in the book. I sunbathed regularly and avoided all the places where there would be unclean air, including the movie theatre where I had so avidly watched foreign films.

Soon my mother discovered another method for curing my illness. She found a Japanese couple who were practising an electrical cure for all ailments. They invented this method and sang the praises of the invention. They placed several square-shaped pads, which were connected to an electric wire, on the spot of the body that was suffering from the particular ailment. Apparently, the low current, when passed through these pads into the human body, cured the illness. I guess my mother couldn't care less whether it was mere "pow pow" or genuine. Anything, to give us the impression that we were doing something, would have been enough.

At the time, my mother was suffering from the symptoms of menopause, so she needed something to make her feel better, too. The mother and daughter, together, trotted off to this clinic regularly.

The couple who ran this clinic did not look like the ordinary Japanese. Both of them were much bigger (wider) in size and were quite cosmopolitan. The wife used to be a famous "shakuhachi" (a Japanese wind instrument, made of bamboo) player and had gone around the world, giving concerts. In the days when one traveled by ship, going around the world was quite a venture. She had a stack of photos which were a record of her past glory. In the photos, she was clad in traditional Japanese costumes, holding the "shakuhachi". The "kimonos" were more colourful than ordinary kimonos and they had long sleeves because they were meant for the stage. She also had dozens of postcards from various countries around the world. I was especially interested in the postcards of Paris. When I looked at the postcard of Notre Dame Cathedral in Paris, I made up my mind that I would definitely visit Paris one day. Mrs. Suzuki was instrumental in determining my future.

Because I did not have to go to work, I stayed idle at home. There were no books to read and nothing to study. I wanted to study English and Chinese, but we could not afford the tuition and I also could not find the teachers. There was a big date tree near the kitchen. It bore beautiful fruit. I picked the fruit and ate it while sunning myself.

The kitchen building had been abandoned because it showed signs of serious decay. My mother cooked outside and washed up in another section of the compound. This house had four sections, all separated. I lived with my sister in one section. One day, I was sitting in my room. My parents were out. My elder sister was at work and my younger sister was at school. The kitchen sat quietly. I had some strange sensation, as if this stillness was a prelude to something drastic. All of a sudden, I heard faint noises as if pebbles were being dropped one by one. Soon the faint noises increased in their volume and became loud. I saw the brick walls of the kitchen disintegrating. The stones started falling rapidly and within a minute, the whole building collapsed. As I watched with my mouth open from astonishment, the whole building lay in ruins and dust rose like the smoke from Aladdin's lamp and disappeared. It was wise of my mother to have stopped using it. The collapse was so quick, if anybody had been in there, he or she would have been crushed to death. After a few minutes of noise, the kitchen lay there silently in ruins, as if nothing had happened.

One day, a marmalade cat walked in out of blue. From his looks I could tell he had lived with a wealthy Chinese family. In China, only very wealthy families could afford pets. Any family less than wealthy would not have had the means to feed an animal—they had to feed themselves first. His coat had the shine that could only be acquired by eating meat. He was sleek and beautiful. I did not know where he came from. He literally came suddenly out of nowhere. Once he came, he did not make any attempt to go back home. He settled in with me. He didn't care about the rest of the family. I gave him a Japanese name—Mimi, the name I once gave to the cat I had to give up. He even responded to the name I gave him. He ate the food I gave, although I can't remember what I gave him and he played joyfully when I played Hide and Seek with him. Just once, he went away for a while and I thought he went back home but he returned.

Beside the room where I lived, there was a vacant room with a concrete floor. One day, in the middle of that room I found a huge scorpion, creeping along the floor. If one gets bitten by this creature, the bite spot swells up like a balloon and one gets very sick. The cat saw it. In a second, he jumped and pounced on the scorpion. He was like a lion in the jungle. He was swift and skilful. The scorpion was dead in no time. I gazed at the corpse of the insect half dazed. Maybe the Mimi I had had years before, came back to protect me in the body of another cat.

Soon after this incident, the cat disappeared. I waited for him for many nights and once, I thought I saw him on the roof of our house. I called out to him, but it was only a shadow. I just hoped that he went back to his original home and had not gotten killed. Perhaps he sensed that Japan would soon surrender and he would not be able to stay with me. He took a part of my heart with him.

Because the kitchen was out of use, my mother had been cooking outside. The method is primitive and was an extension of what we had been doing in Japan. Only instead of "sumi" (burnt wood), we were using compressed coal—something similar to present-day barbecue coals. There was only one stove. So we had to cook the dishes one by one. It was a long, tedious procedure. My elder sister made herself useful, but she had to work, so my mother hired an amah. The previous amah my mother was used to, could not come, so another woman came. She was a stout, succinct woman. It was not only her physical build that was heavyish, but she also gave the impression of being heavy in temperament. Her bodily movement was slow and her response to any question took about two minutes to come. She looked like a bear who was about to awaken from hibernation but was reluctant to do so.

On her third day of work, the amah came with a red swelling, the size of a tennis ball, on her foot. She showed it to my parents and claimed that she had hurt herself in our bathroom and it became infected. My good-natured parents immediately sympathized. They dismissed her and gave her an ample sum of money for medical treatment. Afterwards it dawned on them that she was actually not hurt at our place, but she must have been bitten by a scorpion. Only a scorpion bite would swell up like that. She quit after she got the money.

Most of the Japanese were not treating the Chinese and the Koreans well. They believed that the Japanese were the superior race and could not think that, even if the Chinese and the Koreans had black hair and black eyes just like the Japanese, they were different peoples and their way of life and thinking were just different, not inferior. My mother who was a Korean's wife, naturally, had no prejudice. Whenever she went to Tong Tan Pai Row to do some shopping, there was a particular yancho man who would bring her back home. One day my mother finished shopping at the market, came out and looked for this man. Instead of him, a young boy, who was pulling a yancho behind him, called out to my mother.

"Tai, tai"(madam). The yancho was twice his size. "My father is sick today, so I am working."

My mother knew then that this young boy was the son of the man who usually took her home from the market.

"Tai, Tai, please ride my yancho."

"Oh, no," my mother protested, "I'm much too fat for you. You are too small for me."

"Please, Tai, Tai. If you don't ride, I shall have to pull another Japanese and I don't like other Japanese."

My mother thought this was reasonable. So she got on the yancho and said: "Go slowly. Don't run. Manmandae (slowly)."

When they arrived home, she told the boy to wait. My mother quickly made a package of rice and put some money in an envelope.

"I give you these. Don't work any more today. It's finished. Take your father to a doctor with this money."

When the New Year came, the yancho man put on his New Year clothes and came to our parents' house. He wanted to invite my mother to the New Year's celebration at his house. She did not go, not because she did not want to go to a Chinese house, but she feared that if she had gone and eaten their food, they would have had less to eat.

My mother had a beautiful lace parasol. It could be obtained only in Japan and even in Japan, because of the War, one could no longer buy a luxury item like it. One day, when she got off a yancho, she discovered that she had left it in the yancho. She went to the police and she immediately realized she should have never come. In some countries, where the police are not always the upholders of the law, it is better not to go to the police even if a crime is committed. She deeply regretted that she had come. She quickly retracted her statement.

"I must have left it somewhere else. I don't care about my parasol. I don't want it back."

At the sight of the yancho man who was brought in, she almost screamed. "Please don't beat him. I really don't care about my parasol." She finally said: "I won't leave until you release him."

The policeman said to her: "Madam, why don't you go home? We will look after this matter."

"No", said my mother, "I won't leave until he leaves."

"He will be all right. We will take care of it."

"Promise me not to beat him," my mother insisted.

"No, we won't."

"Are you sure?"

The policeman looked at her hard and said:" Madam, you are a benevolent lady."

My mother repeated for years later: "I wish I had not gone to the police! I wish I had not gone to the police!"

I can't remember when, maybe when we went to the place where my father worked, we were on a train. I remember my mother was wearing a kimono. The train suddenly halted with a jerk and we heard a Japanese man shout in a rough barbarous voice. We went to the window to see what was going on. A middle-aged stocky Japanese man had just hit a young Chinese fellow over the head with a wooden club.

"What do you think you are doing, you idiot!"

Apparently, the Chinese man made some mistake and that was why the train had to stop. Blood was trickling down from the Chinese man's head, which was bowed deeply in obedience before the Japanese. My mother nearly fainted. She ran up and down the aisle begging: "Please, someone stop that beating. Please, please." Her breath was rough from excitement. No one replied. Almost every passenger was standing at the window, holding their breath. I am quite sure, there were among the passengers, some people who felt the same way as we did, but no one would dare protest because it might harm us. I wanted to cry. I hated the cruelty imposed upon us by the authority, at which we could not fight back. I hated the powerlessness of the small ordinary citizen. The injustice imposed upon the powerless deeply hurt me. In that young Chinese man's heart, hatred for the Japanese must have been burning with the fierceness of hellfire. What happened to that wound in his head? What did his mother think?

Chapter XVIII

Japan plodded on and continued to fight alone after Italy and Germany had surrendered. But it was obvious that the War was coming to its end. Everybody, except the Japanese, could almost hear the last gasping breath of Japan. One summer day, a draft paper was delivered to every able-bodied Japanese male in Peking. The red paper, they called it, was an impending death sentence. All the males in the office except Mr. O, who had consumption, were summoned to the front to fight. The only males left were either sick or old Japanese men or Koreans, who, they thought, were not worthy of fighting for the sacred country of Japan.

However, they did draft some young Korean boys because they were desperate. Those young unfortunate Koreans perished in the War without even being recognized as Japanese nationals. They were equal only in death. The injustice and secret is buried and hushed up in the hustle of history.

Mr. Ishii, who once became cross at the mistakes I made when I used the abacus, used to be a journalist. When he was drafted, his wife was expecting a baby and the date of delivery was close. He left me a note, the cry of an innocent victim, who was about to be swept away by the force of history. He poured out his heart to a girl of sixteen. He probably would have cried onto the shoulder of a rock; he needed an outlet for his sorrows. He must have been killed in the battle. He was the kind of nice person to whom misfortune tends to hit. His note said: "Misao is a nice name. If my baby is a girl, I will name her after you. Last night I went out alone to walk around. I looked up to the sky and cried, thinking of my fate."

On August 6, 1945, my father came home from work, pale-faced. The Americans dropped a powerful bomb on Hiroshima. The Japanese were trying to tone it down but a whisper was spreading among the Chinese and the Koreans that it must have been an atom bomb.

"This is something very serious", said my father. Three days later, another atom bomb was dropped on Nagasaki. In the meantime, the Japanese politicians made a great blunder by asking the Soviet Union to intervene for peace. The latter took advantage and declared war on Japan on the 8th of August. The army of the Soviet Union started attacking the Japanese army on the Manchurian border. Later they poured into Manchuria, throwing it into turmoil.

Only the Japanese did not know the facts. All the foreigners in Peking knew that it was a matter of days before Japan's surrender would be made public. My mother secretly informed our nice neighbour. Mrs. Takeda became greatly confused.

"Are you sure?" she repeatedly asked. She just could not believe that Japan would ever lose the War. In her confusion, she even wanted to believe that we were feeding her with false information because we were Koreans. Poor people! They did not do anything wrong. People like the nice neighbours and Mr. Ishii, who were good, had to take the consequences of the folly of the government.

At 12:00, noon, on August 15, 1945, we were told to listen to the broadcast of the Emperor's message. Bad reception interrupted his speech with noises that resembled the surges of waves. He read, with his stiff royal voice, the speech written in the classical style. The broadcast became faint and loud and loud and faint. If we had not known beforehand that this was the Emperor's edict to let the people know that Japan had surrendered, we would have had difficulty in understanding its content. All through the years during the War when despair overtook me, I kept on telling myself: "Anything in this world that begins will eventually end. The War, too, will eventually end." The War did end. I was almost numb with disbelief.

That night, I sat on a stone step and looked up to the sky. I still could not quite believe that I was finally free. My freedom, for which I had so longed, was now a reality. I felt like a bird that was suddenly released from its cage. This sudden freedom froze my senses. I was almost frightened. Trembling with disbelief, I looked up to the dark sky. There was one bright star. I can't remember any other stars. I remember, even unto this day, this big bright star in the black ink of the vast cosmos.

The War did end.

About the Author

Miriam Misao Batts was born in Japan. She was educated at Keisen Jogakuen, the International Academy of the Convent of the Sacred Heart and Sophia University in Tokyo, Japan, where she received a B.Sc in Social Science. From Julius Maximilian University in Wuerzburg, Germany, she earned a Dr. of Philosophy in History. She later studied fashion design at the Lydia Lawrence Fashion Institute in Vancouver, B.C., Canada. She worked as a fashion designer and a doll maker for a while.

In 1984, she became a student of the world-renowned Chinese painter, Johnson Su-sing Chow, studied Fine Arts at U.B.C. for a year and has been studying art. She had given exhibitions and some of her works are in private collections. She also teaches art privately.

Her paintings can be viewed at: HtmlResAnchor www.ccafv.org.

Miriam is also a poet. Her poems have been published in 21 anthologies, including "The Best Poems" of 1998, "The Best Poems and Best Poets" of 2001, 2002 and 2003 by the International Library of Poetry, and "Theatre of the Mind" by Noble House in England. She also published a poetry book, entitled "Passing of the Summer." Her poems can be viewed at www.poetry.com and www.poemsoftheworld.com. She will be in "Who's who" of poets, which will be published by the International Library of Poetry in 2004. She has written articles, both in English and in Japanese, and they have been published in Japan, England and Canada.

She draws enjoyment from another field of art, music. She started taking lessons in piano at the age of 57 and now holds a Grade Ten diploma in piano from the Conservatory of Music in Toronto, Canada. She is married to an Englishman, who is a professor emeritus in medieval German, has a married daughter and lives in B.C., Canada.

ISBN 1-41204430-8